UPLIFTING THOUGHTS
FOR EVERY DAY

"The Kingdom of God is close at hand" (Mt 1:15).

UPLIFTING THOUGHTS FOR EVERY DAY

MINUTE MEDITATIONS FOR EVERY DAY CONTAINING A SCRIPTURE READING, A REFLECTION, AND A PRAYER

By
Father John Catoir

Illustrated

CATHOLIC BOOK PUBLISHING CORP.
New Jersey

CONTENTS

NIHIL OBSTAT: Very Rev. Msgr. James M. Cafone, M.A., S.T.D.
Censor Librorum

IMPRIMATUR: ✛ Most Rev. John J. Myers, J.C.D., D.D.
Archbishop of Newark

The Nihil Obstat and Imprimatur are official declarations that a book or a pamphlet is free of doctrinal or moral error. No implication is contained therein that those who have granted the Nihil Obstat and Imprimatur agree with the contents, opinions or statements expressed.

(T-197)

ISBN 978-1-937913-02-1

© 2007 Catholic Book Publishing Corp., N.J.
Printed in China
www.catholicbookpublishing.com

INTRODUCTION

Be Your Own Best Friend

ONE of the most important things you can do to improve your mental health and your spiritual life is to fill your mind with uplifting thoughts.

Did you know that the thoughts you think always filter down, and become the emotions you feel? Toxic thinking is the cause of most of your emotional pain.

You can eliminate negative thinking, and improve your emotional life by putting on the indomitable will to count your blessings. You can choose to be happy by filling your mind with uplifting thoughts.

The mind only has room for one set of thoughts at a time. If you think good thoughts, the toxic ones won't have any room to fester. Healing begins when you decide to move out of that self-imposed mental swamp.

Stop identifying with your thoughts. You are not your thoughts. You are the observer of your thoughts. When you observe yourself slipping into a dark state of mind, think positively; stay focused on the things that bring you joy and peace.

If you hold on to hurtful memories, they will only make you sick. You have a choice. You can reject them. Decide firmly that you will not let the past drag you down.

Once you stop living inside your own head you can look around, and begin living in the present moment. Listen to the birds; smell the roses. Use your senses to break the spell of gloom and doom.

5

Turn to the Lord, and ask for help. Poisonous thoughts will hang around as long as you take no action to dispel them. Pray for the grace to come into the present moment. Instead of wallowing in the past, or worrying about the future, let your eyes, your ears, your nose, your taste buds, and your sense of touch lead you to that new plateau of freedom called the present moment. Only there can you find relief from all your fears.

Some examples of toxic thinking include: (1) the fear of failure, ("What if I make a bad impression?"); (2) the fear of danger, ("What if someone attacks me?"); (3) the fear of facing the challenge of life, ("What if I ended it all?"). These thoughts are not you, they are toxic invaders. Banish them from your mind, or they will destroy your peace, and possibly end your life.

You don't have to work endlessly through the toxic effects of the past. Once you decide to change, the process can begin. It will take time, but it can be done, provided you persist in your good intentions.

It's never too late to change. I've written this little book as a tool to help you to control your thoughts and live a happier, holier life.

St. Teresa of Avila used to repeat to herself over and over: "Let nothing disturb you; let nothing cause you to fear. God is unchanging love. He will protect you."

With the Lord at your side, you can do all things. Remember the words of Jesus: *"I have told you all these things that your joy may be full" (Jn 15:11).*

Blessings of peace and joy.

Father John Catoir

O NOT let your hearts be troubled. . . . Place your trust in God.

JAN.
1

—Jn 14:1

Being True to Your Inner Self Is Easy

REFLECTION. The late Mother Teresa said: "If you are kind, people may take advantage of you . . . be kind anyway. If you are trusting, people may try to cheat you . . . be trusting anyway. If you are happy, people may become jealous . . . be happy anyway."

This is good advice, coming from a woman who knew the truth and lived it.

PRAYER. *Teach me, Lord, to hear Your voice within me, and to follow Your inspiration.*

 OD is faithful, and will not allow you to be tried beyond your strength.

JAN.
2

—1 Cor 10:13

Persevere in Your Good Intentions; You'll Be Glad You Did

REFLECTION. Did you know that babies teach us a lot about perseverance? For instance, babies can't read books about how to walk. They just keep standing up, and falling down, over and over, until finally they take their first steps, and everyone rejoices with them.

Perseverance pays. Hang in there.

PRAYER. *Help me, Lord, to be more faithful to Your holy Will.*

HE prayer of faith will save the sick person, and the Lord will raise him up.

—Jas 5:15

JAN. 3

It Pays to Trust in the Power of Prayer

REFLECTION. Here is a prayer taken from a confederate soldier's knapsack:

"I asked for strength that I might achieve great things, but I was made weak that I might ask for God's strength. I didn't get exactly what I asked for, but did get everything I hoped for, and today, I feel richly blessed."

PRAYER. *Dear God, give me the grace to be more trusting.*

 N MY anguish I cried out to the Lord and . . . He heard my voice.

—Ps 18:7

JAN. 4

Time Heals All Wounds

REFLECTION. Scripture tells us that love is patient. It is so true. The service of love often takes the form of waiting, which can feel like a slow death at times.

The earth waits for rain, the bud waits for warmth, and the soul waits for a union with God. Healing is yours for the asking.

PRAYER. *Dear Jesus, help me to carry my cross with courage.*

OPE will not be doomed to disappointment, because the love of God has been poured into our hearts through the Holy Spirit. —Rom 5:5

The Love of God Is Your Strength

REFLECTION. Did you know that children do better in school when their parents encourage them to have a hopeful, positive attitude?

Parents have the power to give their children a gift more valuable than anything money can buy, namely the gift of hope and encouragement. A pat on the back goes a long way.

PRAYER. *Lord, help me to feel Your encouragement, as I am encouraging others.*

 ING to the Lord a new song, His praise in the assembly of the saints. —Ps 149:1

Why Not Decide to Be Happy?

REFLECTION. Did you ever stop to think that happiness is a choice? We can actually make up our mind to live joyfully. In fact, the greatest honor you can give to Almighty God, greater than all your mortifications, is to live joyfully because of the knowledge of His love.

God wants you to enjoy your precious life. So cheer up!

PRAYER. *Heavenly Father, give me the grace to choose happiness.*

F I have . . . all the faith to move mountains, but do not have love, I am nothing.

—1 Cor 13:2

7

True Love Is in the Will

REFLECTION. The will says yes or no. Finding a way to work through problems in a marriage can be difficult. Sometimes it is downright infuriating. But once you say yes to love, your life will become easier.

It takes a vow to keep a person on the right path. Don't give up because of bad feelings. True love is in the will.

PRAYER. *Dear Lord, give me the strength to forgive, and to have a sense of humor as I plug along.*

 ELOVED, let us love one another, because love is from God.

—1 Jn 4:7

8

Spiritual Intimacy Is Yours for the Asking

REFLECTION. Prayer is one way to grow closer not only to God but also to those nearest to you. Prayer makes life more bearable, and yes, even more glorious.

Learn how to rest in His love, as you give yourself to God. Be still and know that God loves you.

PRAYER. *Dear God, bring me closer to Your heart of hearts.*

HE Lord takes pleasure in those who fear Him, those who place their hope in His kindness. —Ps 147:11

Enjoy the Lord

REFLECTION. Joseph Cardinal Bernardin once wrote: "The Risen Christ is with you this day. He continues to need you. . . . He needs your hands to continue blessing others. He needs your heart to continue loving those in need."

PRAYER. *Holy Spirit of Love, You are present within me; teach me to enjoy Your presence.*

 RANT them Your protection so that those who love Your Name may rejoice in You. —Ps 5:12

Protect Your Mind from Fear

REFLECTION. St. Peter said, "Grow in the grace and the knowledge of our Lord and Savior Jesus Christ" (2 Pet 3:18). You can do this by blocking out needless fear.

St. Teresa of Avila said, "Let nothing disturb you. Let nothing cause you to fear. God is unchanging love, God alone suffices."

PRAYER. *Jesus, help me to banish all fear, and trust You.*

ET the rivers clap their hands and the mountains shout for joy. Let them sing before the Lord. —Ps 98:8-9

God Is Present in All Creation; Enjoy the View

REFLECTION. Faith opens a thousand eyes. The oceans, the stars, the mountains, and the plains—all reveal the hidden life of God.

Look in faith, and you will see the beauty of God all around you.

PRAYER. *Dear Lord, give me the eyes to see Your invisible presence more clearly.*

 UIDE me in Your truth and instruct me, for You are God, my Savior, and in You I hope all the day long. —Ps 25:5

In You, O Lord, I Find My Peace

REFLECTION. The Lord God is both your pilot and your navigator. Let go of the controls, so He can take over.

He will lift you higher each day, in His own way, and at His own speed.

PRAYER. *Father, I'm learning to trust You more and more; be patient with my restlessness.*

EXALTED be the Lord Who delights to see His servant in peace.

—Ps 35:27

JAN.
13

You Are Loved More Than You Know

REFLECTION. It's true. When someone loves another person, he delights in helping and protecting that person.

The Bible proclaims the truth that God loves each of us with an infinite, unchanging love. This knowledge is a joy forever. Relish it today.

PRAYER. *Dear God, I trust Your love. Fill my soul with joy.*

 PRUDENCE will protect you, and understanding will watch over you.

—Prov 2:11

JAN.
14

Spend Wisely That Your Future May Be Secure

REFLECTION. Fiscal conservatives tend to live longer. Some of them even enjoy life more because they have savings in their old age.

But you will have greater peace than the richest person on earth if you learn to put your trust in the Lord.

PRAYER. *Lord, enable me to place my trust in You, and not in riches.*

WHEN you lie down, you will not be afraid, and on your bed your sleep will be sweet.

JAN. 15

—Prov 3:24

A Clean Conscience Brings Peace of Soul

REFLECTION. Everyone makes mistakes, but those who turn the past over to God's mercy and the future to His loving Providence find peace of soul in the present moment.

Your conscience will rest easy when you forget the past, and enjoy your precious life now.

PRAYER. *Make me into a new creation this day, O Lord.*

 STOP your weeping! She is not dead; she is asleep.

JAN. 16

—Lk 8:52

God Can Perform Miracles in Your Life

REFLECTION. Do not weep for yourself if you are weak. No matter what your faults may be, they are as nothing to the God of Power and Mercy.

The Lord will bring healing if you ask, and the fullness of joy. Turn your life over to Him, and He will deliver you from your misery.

PRAYER. *Thank You for my faith in You, Lord. Help me in my need.*

TRUST the Lord forever, for in Him you have an everlasting Rock.

—Isa 26:4

Lift Up Your Thoughts

REFLECTION. What you sow in your mind, you will reap in your emotions. What you sow in your emotions, you will reap in your actions. And what you sow in your actions, you will reap in your destiny.

Toxic thoughts produce toxic emotions. Focus on the quality of your thoughts. Be your own best friend; control your thoughts.

PRAYER. *Keep me on the straight and narrow, Lord. Help me to control my thinking.*

 TAKE delight in the Lord, and He will grant you what your heart desires.

—Ps 37:4

I Will Live Joyfully, No Matter What

REFLECTION. The teaching of a great 15th-century mystic, named Blessed Julian of Norwich, inspires us this day with true wisdom.

She wrote, "The greatest honor you can give the Almighty God, greater than all your sacrifices and mortifications, is to live joyfully because of the knowledge of His love."

PRAYER. *Dear Holy Spirit, fill my soul with gladness.*

WILL go to the altar of God, to the God of my joy and delight, and I will praise You with the harp, O God, my God. —Ps 43:4

JAN. 19

Praise Is the Highest Form of Prayer

REFLECTION. Jesus said, "Learn from Me, for I am meek and humble of heart" (Mt 11:29). He always turned to the Father to give Him praise, as well as to ask for help.

Give praise and reverence to God each day, and He will reward your heart's desire.

PRAYER. *Heavenly Father, I praise Your Holy Name as I place my needs before You.*

 OUR deeds, O Lord, have caused me to exult; at the works of Your hands I shout for joy. —Ps 92:5

JAN. 20

Be Still and Know That You Are Loved

REFLECTION. From time to time pursue moments of contemplation. Calm down, and become aware of the Lover within you.

St. Paul said, "In Him we live and breathe and have our being" (Acts 17:28). A few seconds each hour is enough to let Him know you care.

PRAYER. *Lord, wipe the mist from my eyes that I may see Your glory.*

EED advice and accept instruction so that your wisdom may increase in the future. —Prov 19:20

JAN. 21

Your Choices Will Define Who You Are

REFLECTION. The ancient philosopher Epictetus gave us some sage advice: "First say to yourself what you should be, and then do what you have to do."

It sounds so simple, but try it. Staying faithful to your noble goals and aspirations takes will-power.

PRAYER. *There's still time for me, Lord, to make my life really meaningful. Give me the grace to keep trying.*

 UR mouths were filled with laughter, and our tongues with songs of joy. —Ps 126:2

JAN. 22

A Cheerful Heart Is a Shield against Adversity

REFLECTION. To develop an attitude of joy one must prepare long in advance. You don't wait for good things to happen in order to be of good cheer.

Decide now to rejoice in all circumstances, and hold on to that intention. Joy will follow in time. Trust me on that.

PRAYER. *Father, lift me above the turmoil of this world; help me to be a cheerful person.*

ESUS said, "Knock, and the door will be opened to you."
—Mt 7:7

Hope Anticipates the Very Best

REFLECTION. The words of Jesus give us the raw material of hope and encouragement. He asks us to trust Him. That means you have to follow His advice to shape a brighter, happier attitude of mind.

Like love, hope is in the will. Put on the will to be more hopeful.

PRAYER. *Lord, I will put on the indomitable will to expect that the best is yet to come.*

 RUST your own judgment, for you have no counselor more reliable for you.
—Sir 37:13

"Know Thyself"

REFLECTION. "We cannot begin to know ourselves until we can see the real reasons why we do the things we do" (Thomas Merton).

Take the time to think about your underlying motives and prejudices. Then pray for the grace to do God's Will in all your decisions.

PRAYER. *I want to be holy in Your sight, O Lord. Tell what I have to do to improve.*

EHOLD, we are now going up to Jerusalem.

—Mk 10:33

Again, Keep Your Hopes High

REFLECTION. God is on your side. How do you know that? You know it because He loves you, and He wants to give you the fullness of joy. He told you that at the Last Supper.

Fill your life with meaning, and trust that with God's help there will be a happy outcome.

PRAYER. *With You at my side, Lord, all things are possible.*

 LL you peoples, clap your hands, shout to God with cries of gladness.

—Ps 47:2

Prayer Is Adoration

REFLECTION. There are four kinds of prayer: petition, thanksgiving, atonement, and adoration. Adoration is the act of rejoicing in the Lord.

Adoration can be as silent as a sunset, or as loud and thundering as Beethoven's "Ode to Joy." Either way adoration feels good.

PRAYER. *Be still, my soul, and let me praise my Lord and my God.*

ESTORE to me the joy of being saved, and grant me the strength of a generous spirit. —Ps 51:14

This Day I Will Purge My Soul of Sadness

REFLECTION. Sadness can always be traced to some cause. Find the cause, and try to eliminate it from your life.

Some things may have to be accepted as unavoidable unhappiness, but everything else can be tweaked and changed for the better. Count your blessings, and all will be well.

PRAYER. *Help me, Lord, to be more courageous when I want to give up and run away.*

 AM confident that I will behold the goodness of the Lord in the land of the living. —Ps 27:13

God Will Lift You Up

REFLECTION. No need to feel left out in the cold. There is always grace. Do not weep for yourself. Self-pity will only bring you down further.

The Lord will lift you up this day; He will revive your drooping spirit.

PRAYER. *I feel Your embrace, O Lord; carry me higher.*

YOU are my help, and in the shadow of Your wings I rejoice.

—Ps 63:8

Feel God's Protection This Day

REFLECTION. I am protected by God's love. Jesus said, "In this world you will have many problems, but be of good cheer for I have overcome the world" (Jn 16:33).

Do not let your soul be troubled. Let the Lord bring you to safe ground.

PRAYER. *Teach me to trust in Your love more and more, O Lord.*

 CREATE in me a clean heart, O God, and renew a resolute spirit within me.

—Ps 51:12

JAN. **30**

If You Have a Joyful Heart, Please Notify Your Face

REFLECTION. Sometimes the emotional connection between our brain and our body is dull. We know intellectually that God loves us at every moment of the day, but we still remain listless.

St. Paul said, "Rejoice always" (Phil 4:4). Just do it, and don't ask so many questions.

PRAYER. *Lord, quicken my spirit that I may live in Your joy more fully.*

ET them offer sacrifices in thanksgiving
and recount His deeds with jubilation.
—Ps 107:22

I Will Give Thanks to the Lord
with All My Heart

REFLECTION. Life is difficult because there are
endless problems to be solved each day. But if
you take them one at a time, you'll get through
just fine.

Love can make it easy, but perfect love can
make it a joy.

PRAYER. *Lord God, bestow on me a grateful
heart, and let me rejoice in Your wonder.*

 HOSE who are righteous will rejoice;
they will exult before God, crying out
with great delight. —Ps 68:4

Every Day Is a Gift from God

REFLECTION. Enjoy your precious life, but not
as an end in itself. Think of heaven as your
true home.

Try not to move too fast today. When you
race, you tend to see so little. Be aware of the
people around you. Rejoice in God's gifts of
life and love.

PRAYER. *Dear Lord, give me the grace to
become more aware of Your wonders all
around me.*

THOSE who dwell at the ends of the earth are awestruck by Your wonders. You call forth songs of joy from sunrise to sunset. —Ps 65:9

FEB.
2

Joy Is Beholding God's Presence in All Creation

REFLECTION. Walt Whitman once wrote, "A single mouse is miracle enough to convert a thousand infidels." Faith opens one's eyes to see miracles in ordinary things.

Everything around us is part of God's design. His glory shines forth everywhere—if only we had the eyes to see!

PRAYER. *Dear God, grant to me an increase of faith that I may see Your glory.*

THE Lord takes delight in His people. . . . Let the saints exult in their glory and sing for joy. —Ps 149:4, 5

FEB.
3

Be a Channel of God's Peace and Relax

REFLECTION. St. Francis of Assisi prayed, "Make me a channel of Your peace. Where there is hatred, let me bring love. . . . Where there is sadness, joy."

Be like St. Francis; know where to go to get the power turned on. Be a carrier of God's Holy Spirit.

PRAYER. *Lord, make me a channel of Your peace.*

EMEMBER the Sabbath and keep it holy.

FEB. 4

—Ex 20:8

Reclaim the Sabbath As a Day of Rest

REFLECTION. Each Sunday, take the time for reflection and prayer. The goal of contemplation is to do nothing; to think nothing. Just rest in God the way a pet rests in the lap of its master.

The idea is to pray without words. Focus on *being* rather than *doing*.

PRAYER. *Lord, I will be still, and know that I am being loved.*

 VERLASTING delights [are] at Your right hand.

FEB. 5

—Ps 16:11b

Enjoy the Spiritual Pleasures

REFLECTION. A grateful heart brings joy to the soul. Be grateful this day. Don't dwell on your losses. Focus on the gift of life, and begin again.

Be grateful if you have known the meaning of true love. Be grateful even if you haven't.

PRAYER. *Dear Lord, thank You for all that I have been given. Teach me to count the blessings.*

CHEERFUL heart is excellent medicine, but a crushed spirit dries up the bones. —Prov 17:22

FEB. 6

"Accept Your Troubles, Com'on Get Happy"

REFLECTION. Judy Garland sang the above song so beautifully.

If you are grieving, you can decide to be miserable for three months, three years, or thirty years. Which is best for you? Focus on the gift of life as best you can, and not the loss of life. It is possible to decide to be happy, even in the most terrible circumstances.

PRAYER. *Dear Lord, thank You for all that I have been given. Again I ask, teach me to count my blessings.*

 OU have taken away my sackcloth and clothed me with joy. —Ps 30:12b

FEB. 7

Ask For Joy; It Is a Divine Gift

REFLECTION. The Lord is preparing you for the banquet of joy. Everything He does is designed to bring you safely home to heaven.

Sometimes he sends a shocking wake-up call; but most times he sends a gentle kiss. Either way it is a gift that can bring you joy.

PRAYER. *Lord, help me to rejoice in all circumstances.*

BEAR one another's burdens, and in this way you will fulfill the law of Christ.
—Gal 6:2

FEB.
8

Friendship Is a Sign of Love

REFLECTION. It pays dividends to promptly reach out to help someone in need. You can solidify old friendships, and make new ones by acts of unexpected kindness.

Think of others, and follow the Golden Rule. It will win you many blessings.

PRAYER. *Father, help me to do unto others that which I would want done unto me.*

 THEREFORE, we love because He first loved us.
—1 Jn 4:19

FEB.
9

Be Kind to Yourself This Day

REFLECTION. "Don't be disturbed because of your imperfections, and always rise up bravely from a fall. Every day make a new beginning" (St. Frances de Sales).

Be your own best friend, because no one can do that for you.

PRAYER. *Lord, help me to be a little kinder to myself. I need to lighten up a little.*

LESSED are the peacemakers, for they will be called children of God.

—Mt 5:9

Make Peace Not War

REFLECTION. This is important, especially in family matters. Set your sights on family unity, and don't let petty bickering erode your joy.

Resentment and impatience can eat away at a person's happiness and destroy family life. Be a peacemaker, even if you are ridiculed for it.

PRAYER. *Father Almighty, deliver us from evil, and liberate me from my pet peeves.*

 ERVE as an example to the believers in your speech and conduct. —1 Tim 4:12

Control Your Tongue

REFLECTION. Don't store up resentments; they will eventually burst out in words and shouts that will inflict pain and wound feelings. Forgive quickly.

At least pray for the grace to let go, and let God be God. Control your speech, and you will be pleasing to the Lord.

PRAYER. *Dear God, I can't do this without a minor miracle. Please help me.*

LESSED are those who hunger and thirst for justice, for they will have their fill.
—Mt 5:6

FEB. 12

Great Causes Require Great Sacrifices

REFLECTION. Abraham Lincoln kept our nation together with words of wisdom like these: "If the union of these States, and the liberties of these people be lost, it is but little to any one man . . . but a great deal to millions of others, and to their posterity."

Now we can thank God we stood the course, but then the Civil War seemed so wasteful.

PRAYER. *Grant me, Lord, the wisdom to know Your Will.*

 N intelligent man remains silent . . . a trustworthy man keeps things hidden.
—Prov 11:12, 13

FEB. 13

To Be Good, Be a Good Listener

REFLECTION. One way to endear yourself to others is to be willing to listen when they need to talk.

You will perform a valuable service by virtually doing nothing except remaining quiet, and showing concern. This will take enormous willpower in many cases, but you will be appreciated more than you know.

PRAYER. *Help me to understand, Lord, that my silence is often the greatest gift I can give.*

S the Father has loved Me, so have I loved you. Remain in My love.

—Jn 15:9

FEB.
14

Happy Valentine's Day

REFLECTION. To love others well, you have to love yourself. Love of self is not self-centered. Rather it is a love that reflects the mystery of God's unchanging love for you.

Don't put yourself down, and don't abuse your body with excessive eating and drinking.

PRAYER. *Help me, Lord, to love myself in the proper way.*

LL things work together for good for those who love Him and who are called according to His purpose.

—Rom 8:28

FEB.
15

You Are So Lovable

REFLECTION. It's true, once you have faith deep enough to realize how much God loves you, you will have to feel good about yourself.

God thinks you are lovable, and He is never wrong.

PRAYER. *Dear Lord, thank You for loving me.*

WILL give you a new heart, and put a new spirit within you.

—Ezek 36:26

FEB. 16

Jesus Is within You

REFLECTION. "Do not look for Jesus apart from yourself. He is not somewhere out here. He is within you" (Mother Teresa of Calcutta).

We focus too often on the material world around us and ignore the invisible world of spiritual treasures. Divine powers reside within you.

PRAYER. *Help me to look within myself, Lord.*

 AVE no fear of sudden terror. . . . The Lord will be your assurance.

—Prov 3:25, 26

FEB. 17

Helplessness Is Not Hopelessness

REFLECTION. Psychiatrist Dr. Abraham Low said, "Just because you feel helpless about something doesn't mean there is no hope. Feelings are not facts."

The fact is that you have the power of God within you. Jesus said that prayer can move mountains (Mt 21:21). Take Him at His word and pray with assurance.

PRAYER. *Jesus, teach me to put all my hope in You.*

F YOU forgive others . . . your heavenly Father will also forgive you.

—Mt 6:14

FEB. 18

Be Merciful

REFLECTION. Here is a formula for being unlikable: hold on to your grudges, never forget a criticism, and always resent those who hurt your feelings.

Instead imitate Jesus Who said, "Forgive them, Father, for they know not what they do" (Mt 23:34).

PRAYER. *Dear Jesus, You not only forgave Your enemies, You made excuses for them. I need a lot of help to get to that level.*

 E has anointed us and marked us with His seal and given us the Spirit in our hearts.

—2 Cor 1:22

FEB. 19

We Are All Linked

REFLECTION. Because of a deep sense of Christian community, the harmony of the group is a prime attribute.

Be more group-minded than self-centered. You'll feel a lot better.

PRAYER. *Holy Spirit, let me use my gifts and talents for others.*

IVE thanks in all circumstances; for this is the Will of God for you in Christ Jesus. —1 Thes 5:18

FEB.
20

The Duty of Delight

REFLECTION. Given all the gifts that God has bestowed on you, it is almost rude to be a complainer. Dorothy Day called this gratitude "the duty of delight."

Gratitude always makes you feel better.

PRAYER. *I thank You, Father, for my being and my life.*

 ET us therefore cast aside the works of darkness and put on the armor of light. —Rom 13:12

FEB.
21

This Lent Reject Every Trace of Envy

REFLECTION. Envy is sadness over the good fortune of another. Learn to spot that sadness when it arises in your heart, and then stamp it out.

Focus on your own unique qualities, not what you lack. Do not allow sadness to rule your heart.

PRAYER. *Lord, let me praise You when I resent the good fortune of others.*

HERE your treasure is, there will your heart also be.

—Mt 6:21

FEB. 22

Set Your Heart on Heaven

REFLECTION. It is good to enjoy your precious life, but not as an end in itself.

Pope John Paul II said, "It is not wrong to want to live better; what is wrong is a style of life which is directed toward having, rather than being. . . ."

PRAYER. *Let my heart be truly Yours, Lord.*

 HAVE learned to be content with whatever I have. I know how to live with little, and I know how to live with plenty.

—Phil 4:11, 12

FEB. 23

Be Content

REFLECTION. A peaceful spirit is attainable.

All you need is the will to count your blessings, the wisdom to accept the things you cannot change, and the courage to change the things you can.

PRAYER. *Holy Spirit, console me, comfort me, and give me peace of soul.*

OVE your enemies, do good to those who hate you.

—Lk 6:27

FEB. 24

Forgiveness Is a Divine Calling

REFLECTION. John Kennedy once said, "Forgive your enemies, but never forget their names." This is wisdom, but Jesus challenged us to love our enemies.

This does not mean that we can allow terrorists to have their way in the world. The evil tyrant must be stopped, and then forgiven.

PRAYER. *Father, forgive them for they know not what they do, but protect our soldiers in the process.*

 ET us then pursue the ways that lead to peace and mutual edification.

—Rom 14:19

FEB. 25

Pride and Prejudice Can Destroy Your Peace

REFLECTION. We all have a tendency to be wary of people who are different, but with a little effort we can look for the many things we have in common.

The more we accept our own shortcomings, the easier it will be to accept others.

PRAYER. *O Lord, help me to love my neighbor.*

Y mouth is filled with Your praises as I relate Your glory all day long.
—Ps 71:8

FEB.
26

Prayer Is Being Happy with God

REFLECTION. "Prayer is an aspiration of the heart. It is a simple glance directed to heaven.

"It is a cry of gratitude and love in the midst of trial, as well as joy" (St. Theresa of Lisieux).

PRAYER. *Lord, I share in Your happiness, and I delight in Your joy.*

F YOU abide in Me and My words abide in you, you may ask for whatever you wish, and it will be done for you.
—Jn 15:7

FEB.
27

Expect God to Answer Your Prayer

REFLECTION. Even if you don't know what to ask for, the Lord knows what you need. He loves you better than you love yourself.

Live on a higher level of faith. God's love is real.

PRAYER. *Lord, teach me to pray, teach me how to accomplish Your Will.*

VEN if he stumbles, he will never fall headlong.... For the Lord loves the just, and He will not forsake His faithful ones. —Ps 37:24-28

FEB. 28

Live Up to Your Ideals

REFLECTION. What defines your character? Are you basically selfish with some flashes of charity; or are you truly humble and loving.

Do the right thing, and don't think so much about yourself.

PRAYER. *Give me wisdom, Lord, and give me strength to do the kind thing.*

HAT is man that You are mindful of him, or the son of man that You care for him? —Ps 8:5

FEB. 29

Purpose of Life

REFLECTION. Many people wonder about the purpose of life. Why are we here? Where are we going? They fail to realize, Lord, that You are our origin and destiny.

PRAYER. *Lord, help me to respond to Your love for me by following Your holy Will.*

WILL restore you to health and heal your wounds, says the Lord. **MAR. 1**

—Jer 30:17

Pray, and You Will Be Healed

REFLECTION. Being a caregiver, or a volunteer in difficult circumstances requires great spiritual effort. It also requires physical and psychological strength.

Take care of yourself, so that you can be an effective instrument of God's love.

PRAYER. *I pray for the grace, O Lord, to perform deeds of mercy with courage.*

 F you do good to those who do good to you, what credit is that to you? Even sinners do as much. **MAR. 2**

—Lk 6:33

We Are Called to Charity

REFLECTION. A family is a community, which leaves the front door open wide enough to receive all who need love and protection.

To serve the Lord well, keep the door of your heart open to the needs of others.

PRAYER. *Dear Lord, make me more sensitive. I tend to be selfish too often.*

ANYONE who has two coats must share with the person who has none.
—Lk 3:11

MAR. 3

Clothe the Naked, Visit the Sick

REFLECTION. You may not be able to help the poor in Haiti or Africa, but you can do a little here at home to help the homeless.

Look for ways to be there for others. Every little bit helps.

PRAYER. *Lord, be my guide in these matters.*

LET us . . . with perseverance run the race that lies ahead of us, with our eyes fixed on Jesus.
—Heb 12:1, 2

MAR. 4

Life Is a Long Distance Race; Take It Easy

REFLECTION. Some people put too much pressure on themselves. They are so afraid of failing that they spend their energy recklessly trying "not to fail."

Don't end up weak and drained; there is a better way to live your life.

PRAYER. *Almighty God, help me to slow down.*

WILL not leave you orphans; I will come to you. In a little while, the world will no longer see Me, but you will see Me. Because I live, you also will live.

—Jn 14:18, 19

You Are Never Alone

REFLECTION. Some people feel lost and overwhelmed, but feelings are not facts. God is near; if only they could believe that the Lord will save them.

There is always someone there to help. God even sends His Angels when you ask.

PRAYER. *Jesus, my Lord and my God, keep me under Your wing.*

 EEP] in mind the words of the Lord Jesus who Himself said, "It is more blessed to give than to receive."

MAR. 6
—Acts 20:35

Take Care of Yourself

REFLECTION. First you must take care of yourself. Keep your mind free of toxic thinking. Don't put yourself down. Then think of others, and enjoy the blessing of being a cheerful giver.

To love yourself is to open your heart to the needs of others.

PRAYER. *Dear God, I know that generosity is a sign of gratitude; help me to be grateful.*

39

O YOU not know that your body is **MAR.** the temple of the Holy Spirit . . . and that you are not your own?

7

—1 Cor 6:19

Respect Your Body As a God-Given Gift

REFLECTION. Good athletes must strive to win, but in the process they must also respect their own bodies, minds, and spirits as gifts from God.

In that way, they will treat themselves and their opponents with respect.

PRAYER. *Keep me from taking my health for granted, Lord.*

———————

 OVE bears all things, believes all things, **MAR.** hopes all things, endures all things.

8

—1 Cor 13:7

Stay the Course

REFLECTION. An Irish Prayer:
May your neighbors respect you . . .
Trouble neglect you . . .
The Angels protect you . . .
And heaven accept you.

PRAYER. *Dear Lord, above all, grant me the grace of final perseverance.*

CT justly and love mercy, and walk humbly with your God.

—Mic 6:8

Humility Is Truth

REFLECTION. "If you think going to church makes you a Christian, you probably also think that sitting in a garage will make you a car" (Garrison Keillor).

Face the facts, it takes love and humility to keep you from becoming an egotistical bore.

PRAYER. *Lord, help me to face the truth about myself.*

AITH is the assurance of what we hope for and the conviction about things that cannot be seen.

—Heb 11:1

Skepticism Puts Out the Fire of Hope

REFLECTION. The skeptic says, "The world is in such a mess—what good is religion?" You can also say, "Lots of people are dirty—what value is soap?"

But neither religion nor soap can do any good if it is not used.

PRAYER. *Lord, increase my faith.*

GOD is our refuge and our strength. . . . Therefore, we will not be afraid.

—Ps 46:2-3

Know That the Lord Is Your Protection

REFLECTION. Ask yourself: Why has my life lasted this long? The answer is: because an invisible power sustains you.

But why weren't you taken years ago? Because you still have a job to do that no one else can do. Have the courage to do your duty.

PRAYER. *Lord, I know my life comes from You. Help me to carry out my purpose.*

 YOU will weep and mourn while the world rejoices. You will be sorrowful, but your grief will turn into joy.

—Jn 16:20

Pain and Sorrow Are Part of Life

REFLECTION. Without the experience of pain, you can never really know the full meaning of joy.

You can learn to smile at your pain if you see it as a prelude to endless joy.

PRAYER. *Remove the cup of pain from my lips, O Lord, and ready my soul for eternal happiness.*

O NOT let your hearts be troubled; be not afraid.

—Jn 14:27

Faith Is the Conviction of Things Not Seen

REFLECTION. Here is a quote found carved into the wall of a Nazi concentration camp:

"I believe in the sun even when it is not shining. . . . I also believe in God even when He is silent."

PRAYER. *Lord, I believe; help me in my unbelief.*

 OTHING] will be able to separate us from the love of God in Christ Jesus our Lord.

—Rom 8:39

Tap into Your Higher Power

REFLECTION. Sometimes you may feel alone and abandoned. It doesn't matter because feelings are not facts. The Lord is closer than you know.

Learn to live by faith, and not by feelings. In that way you will rise above the misery of this life.

PRAYER. *Dear God, be my strength and my joy, especially when I'm feeling blue.*

WAS hungry and you gave me something to eat; . . . a stranger and you welcomed me. —Mt 25:35

Be a Good and Gracious Host

REFLECTION. This is an unsafe world, and we have to be careful. Nevertheless, the welcome mat should never disappear from your doorstep.

Once you know that the stranger is not a threat, be gracious. If you do not feel safe, however, be cautious. Better safe than sorry.

PRAYER. *Jesus, I need You to guide me in discerning Your Will.*

ESUS said, "Come to Me, all you who are weary, and overburdened, and I will give you rest." —Mt 11:28

Rest in the Lord

REFLECTION. Try not to live inside your own head. Fear and self-pity are signs of a weak faith.

Jesus says, "Do not be afraid." If you can't manage to do that, come to the Lord quickly, and entrust yourself to His holy care. He will do for you what you cannot do for yourself.

PRAYER. *I need You, Lord, now more than ever.*

HE LED forth His people with rejoicing, His chosen ones with exultation.
—Ps 105:43

MAR. 17

Happy St. Patrick's Day

REFLECTION. This day is a great day for partying; be careful about excessive drinking. Pray for those who abuse their bodies with alcohol.

There are many ways of enjoying life, ways that are good and noble. Make this day a happy one; live it in the Lord.

PRAYER. *Lord, remind me that in Your presence I will find the fullness of joy, not "in a bottle."*

A TRUE friend is one at all times, and a brother is born to render help in time of need.
—Prov 17:17

MAR. 18

Charity Begins at Home

REFLECTION. If you were in need for some reason, wouldn't you want someone to come to your assistance? Then go, and do likewise.

Maybe one of your own family members is in need right now. Help the one who needs the most help; do it today.

PRAYER. *Lord, You love a cheerful giver; free me from selfish isolation.*

HOEVER loves God must also love his brother.

—1 Jn 4:21

Do No Harm

REFLECTION. Pope John Paul II wrote: "To do harm, to promote violence and conflict in the name of religion is a terrible contradiction and an offense against God."

Do no harm. Be kind to your brethren. Pray for the conversion of evildoers.

PRAYER. *Fill me, Lord, with Your Holy Spirit of Love.*

HOSE who trust in Him will understand truth, and the faithful will dwell with Him in love.

—Wis 3:9

A Happy Hour Is Not Always a Holy Hour

REFLECTION. In today's world there is so much pressure on everyone that people often turn to alcohol and drugs for relief. But too much relief leads to trouble.

Be happy in the Lord, and enjoy the precious gift of life. Try to do it without a hangover.

PRAYER. *I rejoice in You, O Lord. You give me the will to stay clean and sober.*

HEN [Jesus] appeared to more than five hundred of the brethren . . . last of all, He appeared to me.

MAR.
21

—1 Cor 15:6, 8

Seeing the Face of Christ

REFLECTION. St. Paul did not see Jesus' face until he was privileged to see His holy face after Jesus ascended into heaven. Whether it was an apparition or a dream we don't know.

Faith can enable us to see the face of Christ in our neighbor.

PRAYER. *Dear Jesus, grant that I may one day see You face to face.*

HEN Jesus saw with what great understanding he had spoken, He said to him, "You are not far from the Kingdom of God." —Mk 12:34

MAR.
22

In His Will You Will Find Your Peace

REFLECTION. Christian faith and obedience lead us to the fullness of life in the Kingdom.

St. Catherine of Siena understood this when she said, "All the way to heaven is heaven."

PRAYER. *Lord, make me worthy of the joys of heaven, and let them begin here and now.*

EFORE your very eyes Jesus Christ was clearly presented. **MAR.**

—Gal 3:1 **23**

The Eucharist Is a Holy Gift; Do Not Neglect It

REFLECTION. We do not need a physical miracle to convince us of the presence of the Lord in the Eucharist.

God gives us the faith and love to discern this wonderful truth. Do not be unbelieving, but believe.

PRAYER. *Holy Lord, may I always rejoice in the gift of Your presence in the Eucharist.*

 OLLOW Me, and I will make you fishers of men. **MAR.**

—Mt 4:19 **24**

You Are Called to Be a Saint

REFLECTION. Since we are all called to be Saints, it follows that you will also be called upon to suffer from time to time. Love leads to service, and service leads to the cross.

Try not to run away from the cross. It is not a form of punishment; it is often a badge of honor.

PRAYER. *Lord Jesus, help me to carry my cross with courage.*

THE Word became flesh and dwelt among us.

—Jn 1:14

The Mother of God

REFLECTION. From the beginning Christians called Mary "the Mother of God." For Jesus was not merely the Son of Mary; He was God Incarnate, the Savior of mankind.

PRAYER. *Father, You made Mary the Mother of our Divine Savior. Help me to cooperate with Your grace and be saved.*

THE tax collector . . . would not even raise his eyes to heaven. Rather, he kept beating his breast as he said, "God, be merciful to me, a sinner."

—Lk 18:13

Humility Is Sweet

REFLECTION. The Pharisees were proud and haughty. Jesus was angry with them. He ridiculed them repeatedly.

When the lowly tax collector thought himself to be unworthy, he stood afar off, beating his breast and saying, "Be merciful to me a sinner." Jesus rewarded him for his humility.

PRAYER. *Lord Jesus, help me to imitate the humility of the tax collector.*

LESSED are those who have not seen and yet have come to believe.

—Jn 20:29

Walk by Faith

REFLECTION. Nothing is more disappointing to the Lord than to see some people demanding visible signs in order for them to believe in the Gospel.

"Whoever believes has everlasting life" (Jn 6:47).

PRAYER. *Lord, I believe. Let me walk by faith in spite of my tendency to be doubtful at times.*

 NLESS you change and become like little children, you will never enter the Kingdom of heaven. —Mt 18:3

Many Are Called, But Few Are Chosen

REFLECTION. Sacred Scripture shows us the standard of good and evil.

We learn from experience that the values of this world are very different from God's standards.

PRAYER. *Heavenly Father, deliver me from evil; help me to do Your Will in all circumstances.*

EN of Galilee, why are you standing there looking up into the sky?
—Acts 1:11

Actions Speak Louder Than Words

REFLECTION. Give God His due. Do not merely meditate on His words. Perform good deeds to give God praise and glory.

In that way, you will produce an abundance of good fruit.

PRAYER. *Give me the grace, Lord, not only to hear Your Word but also to act on it.*

———————

OW great and wonderful are Your works, Lord, God Almighty! Just and true are Your ways.
—Rev 15:3

Enjoy the Lord in the Glory of His Creation

REFLECTION. The Angels bow before the Lord, and the Saints praise His holy Name.

All creation manifests His wondrous deeds. Be happy in His presence.

PRAYER. *Lord, grant me the grace to worship You in spirit and truth by living joyfully.*

AN'S greatest happiness is to be **MAR.** glad and do well. . . . And when we eat and drink and find satisfaction **31** in all our labors, this is a gift of God. —Eccl 3:12-13

God Wants You to Enjoy Life

REFLECTION. The key to enjoying life is to enjoy it not as an end in itself, but as a prelude to eternal happiness.

Eternal joy begins now.

PRAYER. *Holy Spirit, teach me how to be spiritually and emotionally happy.*

 E ON guard against false prophets. . . . **APR.** By their fruits you will know them. —Mt 7:15, 16 **1**

Don't Be a Fool on This Day

REFLECTION. A Chinese garden is an artistic arrangement of stone and tiny pools sprinkled with lovely flowers. Our life is like a garden when we sprinkle it with small acts of kindness.

Only a fool destroys his own garden with acts of meanness.

PRAYER. *Dear God, make me an instrument of Your love.*

EALTH hastily acquired will dwindle away, but when amassed little by little, it will increase.

APR. 2

—Prov 13:11

Build Up Your Treasures in Heaven

REFLECTION. The more you give away in this life, the more you store up for eternity.

The little gifts of praise and kindness we give to those we meet, all build up our treasury.

PRAYER. *Holy Spirit, help us to be generous in little ways this day.*

 OU are precious in my sight.

APR. 3

—Isa 43:4

You Are One of a Kind

REFLECTION. God sees you as His unique creation. Your body is a wonderful, integrated composition of organs and systems.

You have been given many gifts and talents. Your personality and your good intentions are wonderful to behold. You have so much to be grateful for.

PRAYER. *Thank You, Lord, for loving me as though I am Your only child.*

OUR light must shine so that it can be seen by others; this will enable them to observe your good works and give praise to your Father in heaven.

APR. 4

—Mt 5:16

You Are a Light in This World

REFLECTION. A three-thousand-year-old Chinese proverb says:

"It is better to light one candle than to curse the darkness."

PRAYER. *Dear Lord, help me to really make a difference in the lives of others by carrying Your light into the world.*

 HIS is the fast I choose: . . . sharing your bread with the hungry, and bringing the homeless and poor into your house.

APR. 5

—Isa 58:6-7

The Bread of Angels Will Transform You

REFLECTION. Begin being a Saint today. Receive the Eucharist with a happy heart. Be grateful.

The past has brought you where you are today. From now on be the Saint you want to be.

PRAYER. *Dear Lord, help me to see You in the homeless and the outcast.*

THEREFORE, if the Son sets you free, you then will truly be free.

—Jn 8:36

APR.
6

Jesus Died on a Cross for You

REFLECTION. When life is overwhelming don't give up. Be patient. Be confident. God will come through for you.

Difficulties are part of life. Carry your cross with courage.

PRAYER. *Lord, I need the gift of patient endurance. Thank You for Your gift of love.*

 I WILL see you again, and your hearts will rejoice, and no one shall deprive you of your joy.

—Jn 16:22

APR.
7

Make This Day Meaningful

REFLECTION. When Lent is over, the joy increases. If you love God and want to please Him live each day joyfully.

This very act of honoring God with your joy will give your life great meaning. Joy is your vocation.

PRAYER. *Father in heaven, You are my happiness. You are my life.*

" HY do you look among the dead for the One Who is alive? He is not here. He has been raised."

—Lk 24:5-6

Alleluia, He Is Risen

REFLECTION. These words announced the greatest event in human history, the Resurrection of Jesus from the dead.

Let us rejoice and be glad today and forever.

PRAYER. *Jesus, You lead us to eternal glory. Thank You for Your eternal love.*

S GOD'S chosen ones, holy and beloved, put on compassion, kindness, humility, gentleness, and patience.

—Col 3:12

Let the Risen Christ Give You a Gentle Heart

REFLECTION. If you have the Lord in you, His love will overflow to others.

Volunteer at a hospital. Call a sick friend. Tell a family member you love him or her. Your deeds will flow from a loving soul.

PRAYER. *Father, help me to be another Christ.*

E persistent . . . whether in season or out of season.

—2 Tim 4:2

By Sticking to Any Project, You Will Prevail

REFLECTION. Your persistence may be all that is needed to complete some noble project.

Your efforts may be all that it takes to finish an important job that will make this a better world.

PRAYER. *Lord in heaven, help me to endure and persevere in my good intentions.*

 EFEND the rights of the lowly and the poor. Rescue the wretched and the needy.

—Ps 82:3-4

Hold Onto Hope

REFLECTION. If you can give downhearted persons reason to hope, you can transform their sorrow into joy.

The dark cloud of fear will dissipate, and they will feel renewed.

PRAYER. *Spirit of love and encouragement, empower me to build up rather than to tear down.*

EALTH and fitness are better than gold, and a strong body is better than countless riches.

APR.
12

—Sir 30:15

Take Care of Your Body

REFLECTION. Body, mind, and spirit all work together in harmony. Poor eating habits can lead to poor health, obesity, and eventually to a breakdown of mind and spirit.

To stay trim, discipline yourself; good nutrition takes planning. Take care of your health.

PRAYER. *Jesus, make my mind strong enough to take care of my body.*

 O NOT base your judgment on appearances; judge according to what is right.

APR.
13

—Jn 7:24

Do Not Pull Up a Weed Too Quickly

REFLECTION. "A weed is a plant whose virtues have not yet been discovered" (Ralph Waldo Emerson). Malicious gossip is like pulling up a rose before it blooms.

Be careful not to participate. The person you are condemning may be a Saint in a distressing disguise.

PRAYER. *Lord, teach me to keep from judging people too quickly.*

O MATTER how many years you may live, you should enjoy all of them.
—Eccl 11:8

APR. 14

Enjoy Your Precious Life

REFLECTION. Enjoy life, not as an end in itself, but as a divine gift. Jesus said, "I have told you these things so that . . . your joy may be complete" (Jn 15:11).

Take Him at His word and enjoy your life.

PRAYER. *Thank You, Lord, for all the love I have been privileged to receive.*

 TORE up treasure for yourselves in heaven, where neither moth nor rust destroys and where thieves cannot break in and steal.
—Mt 6:20

APR. 15

Find Joy in Christ's Words

REFLECTION. Jesus taught us to find joy, not by looking for it, but by listening to His words in a spirit of humble surrender.

Enjoyment sought for its own sake is a self-centered pursuit. Joy is more a by-product of our intimacy with God.

PRAYER. *Dear Jesus, purify my mind that I may seek first Your Kingdom. I am not sure what that actually means, but I will put my trust in Your intimate presence; and You will guide me.*

THOSE who plan good are loyal and faithful. Diligent labor always yields profit. —Prov 14:22-23

Competition Improves the Human Spirit

REFLECTION. By competing with others we become physically stronger, mentally brighter, and spiritually wiser.

Stay in the human race; excel in giving glory to God.

PRAYER. *Holy Spirit, help me to stay active in working for God's glory.*

YOU desire sincerity of heart; and You endow my innermost being with wisdom. —Ps 51:8

Why Are Our Soldiers Honored?

REFLECTION. Soldiers are honored because they are prepared to die to save others. Jesus does not condemn soldiers who fight in a just war.

A soldier does not hate those who oppose him in battle. They are public enemies of his nation and must be defeated. It is his duty to defend others.

PRAYER. *Jesus, help me to love my personal enemies and to pray for them.*

O ONE can have greater love than to lay down his life for his friends.

—Jn 15:13

APR.
18

Soldiers Deserve Honor

REFLECTION. We honor soldiers because they are ready to lay down their lives to protect us.

The same is true for law enforcement officers.

PRAYER. *Jesus, help me to appreciate the sacrifices of those who defend us.*

 NTRUST your cares to the Lord, and He will uphold you; He will never allow the righteous to waver.

—Ps 55:23

APR.
19

Surrender Control and Let God Handle Things

REFLECTION. Trusting God will relieve you of a heavy burden. You do not have to force a particular outcome.

Let the Lord bring about the "right" outcome, whatever that might be.

PRAYER. *Dear Jesus, I find it so hard to let go; give me the strength to relax my grip and to place my trust in You.*

EJOICE with those who rejoice; weep with those who weep.

—Rom 12:15

APR. 20

Accept Others As They Are

REFLECTION. People always say, "Don't cry" to those experiencing sorrow. But "don't cry" can mean "I'm too uncomfortable when you show your feelings."

It's better to say, "Go ahead and cry, I'm here at your side to comfort you."

PRAYER. *Lord of life, teach me how to be a true friend to those in need.*

"HICH of those three . . . was a neighbor to the man?" . . . "The one who showed him mercy."

—Lk 10:36, 37

APR. 21

Love the Stranger

REFLECTION. The parable of the Good Samaritan is a lesson in charity. The traveler was robbed, beaten, and left for dead. The Samaritan took him to an inn and paid his bill.

Being a neighbor to a stranger is a way of showing the love of God.

PRAYER. *Dear Jesus, help me to be a good Samaritan to those in desperate need.*

THOSE who wait for the Lord . . . shall run and not be weary.

—Isa 40:31

APR.
22

Keep Your Thoughts Grounded in Faith

REFLECTION. Every positive, uplifting thought you hold in mind becomes a prayer.

Choose the life-affirming words of Jesus as your guide through life. Do not be afraid.

PRAYER. *Dear Lord, I will wait on Your word, and renew my strength in Your promises.*

KEEP the Lord always before me, for with Him at my right hand I will never fall. Therefore, my heart is glad and my soul rejoices.

—Ps 16:8-9

APR.
23

Say Yes to Your Own Happiness

REFLECTION. The willingness to receive the gift of God's love and joy is a necessary prelude to happiness both in this world and forever in the next.

Be your own best friend.

PRAYER. *Dear God, teach me how to avoid being my own worst enemy. Teach me self-love.*

CLOTHE yourselves with the new self created in God's image, in the way of uprightness and holiness that belong to the truth. —Eph 4:24

You Are a New Creation

REFLECTION. "Know thyself." To be made in God's image is to reflect that all-powerful image to all those around you.

At the deepest level you are holy, within the holiness of God.

PRAYER. *Father, You are my maker and I am Your child. Help me to know my purpose and destiny.*

DO NOT deprive yourself of the good things today. —Sir 14:14

Don't Postpone Joy

REFLECTION. Make some time for your brain and your body to recuperate from the stress of life. Find new ways to be more playful, but don't turn play into work. "Let go and let God [be God]."

PRAYER. *Lord, help me to smell the roses and enjoy the children at play.*

H E guides the humble in what is right and teaches them the path to follow.

—Ps 25:9

APR. 26

Kindness Is Your Best Quality

REFLECTION. Most of us know when we are being used. Be kind, but be careful.

Jesus went so far as to make excuses for His executioners; He said, "They do not know what they are doing" (Lk 23:34).

PRAYER. *Father, help me to excel in kindness, even if it opens me to being hurt once in a while.*

G OD has made me laugh and all who hear of it will laugh with me.

—Gen 21:6

APR. 27

Your Sense of Humor Is Your Best Asset

REFLECTION. There are enough tensions in life without compounding them. You will be much better off if you laugh more and cry less.

Life is too short to neglect the gift of laughter.

PRAYER. *Lord, teach me how to enjoy my life more.*

YOU are a letter from Christ entrusted to our care, a letter written not with ink but with the Spirit of the living God, and written . . . on tablets of the human heart. —2 Cor 3:3

Your Whole Life Is Like a Sermon

REFLECTION. Your actions speak louder than your words. Christ lives in you, and if you let Him out, He will use you as people flock to those who are willing to listen.

Become a good listener and you'll never be lonely again.

PRAYER. *Dear Jesus, I give You my life; do with me as You will.*

DO NOT be conquered by evil, but conquer evil with good. —Rom 12:21

You Are a Force for Good

REFLECTION. Every individual is a unique gift created to help make this a better world. Your community needs the gifts that only you can give.

Constructive action on your part can improve the world around you. Why not be a powerful force for good?

PRAYER. *Lord, help me to overcome evil with my good actions.*

HARM is deceptive and beauty is fleeting.

—Prov 31:30

APR. 30

Beware of Wolves in Sheep's Clothing

REFLECTION. Thieves all have the same goal. They try to get you to trust them; then they strike.

They can take a lot of time being charming, building up your trust, but once they have it, they act swiftly and then disappear. Be on guard.

PRAYER. *Lord, teach me to be as wise as a serpent, and as simple as a dove. Deliver me from evil.*

 ITH everlasting love, I will have compassion on you.

—Isa 54:8

MAY 1

Talk to God Daily, He Really Likes to Hear from You

REFLECTION. The only way to pray well is to pray often. It makes God happy when you smile at Him, whisper sweet nothings to Him. It sounds corny but it's true.

PRAYER. *Lord, forgive my tendency to take You for granted. I really do love You.*

VERY good tree bears good fruit. . . . A good tree cannot bear bad fruit.

—Mt 7:17, 18

MAY 2

By Their Fruits You Will Know Them

REFLECTION. A healthy fruit tree will produce an abundance of good fruit. A spiritual healthy person will bear spiritual fruit for eternity.

A bad tree only produces bad fruit. You decide.

PRAYER. *Jesus, You are the vine and I am only one of the branches; bless my life with a bountiful harvest of spiritual fruitfulness.*

 LESSED are the merciful, for they will obtain mercy.

—Mt 5:7

MAY 3

Someone Needs Your Mercy Today

REFLECTION. Your readiness to show forth a spirit of forgiveness will have a ripple effect. You will touch many lives by forgiving one person.

You are anointed, so forget your feelings and go forth. Say yes I will forgive because the Lord asks it.

PRAYER. *Dear Jesus, make my heart like unto Thine; fill me with Your tender love.*

ALL you need to do is say "Yes" if you mean "Yes" and "No" if you mean "No." —Mt 5:37

If You Keep It Simple You Will Please the Lord

REFLECTION. Many self-help groups teach their members to keep it simple. No fancy stuff. No spin. No Denial.

Webster's Dictionary defines the word 'simple' as being free from guile and deception. Yes or No.

PRAYER. *Keep me, Lord, from being cunning. Teach me how to keep it simple.*

REFRAIN from anger and turn away from wrath; do not fret—it does nothing but harm. —Ps 37:8

Being Kind to Yourself Will Pay Dividends

REFLECTION. By letting go of anger and forgiving others you will save yourself from needless misery and frustration. Harboring a grudge is emotionally stressful.

"Refrain from anger," and do yourself a favor.

PRAYER. *God of mercy and love, take away my spirit of revenge.*

HETHER you eat or drink, or **MAY** whatever you do, do everything for the glory of God.

—1 Cor 10:31

6

Be Humble and Give God the Glory

REFLECTION. There are many people who spend their lives trying to steal the limelight, and prove their superiority. Don't be like that.

Be humble and give God the glory.

PRAYER. *Dear Lord, teach me the truth that You are everything and I am nothing.*

 HE wonders of the Lord can neither be **MAY** diminished nor increased, nor are they possible to fathom.   —Sir 18:6

7

Friendship With Us Is One of God's Greatest Wonders

REFLECTION. Friendship heightens the joys of prosperity, and softens the sorrows of adversity.

Be a friend to God, and He will be a friend to you.

PRAYER. *Dear Lord, a friend is often the best medicine. Help me to make You a faithful friend.*

THE Lord is the stronghold of my life; of whom should I be afraid? —Ps 27:1

God Is Protecting You Right Now

REFLECTION. You are not alone for God is always with you.

You are bearing good fruit for God is supporting you. You will persevere for God is sustaining you.

PRAYER. *Dear Lord, I know You are with me; help me to trust You more and more.*

———————

WHEN you call upon Me and come and pray to Me, I will hear you. —Jer 29:12

Your Prayer Touches the Lord Immediately

REFLECTION. As you hold God close to you in mind and memory—even though you feel apart—He responds to your love.

Pray with confidence.

PRAYER. *Jesus, in You I live and breathe and have my being. Never let me be parted from You.*

HERE are times when your recovery will be in the hands of a physician.

—Sir 38:13

Trust the Divine Physician

REFLECTION. People live longer today because of advanced medical science, but God is the one who gives the doctors the skills they need when they are working.

Always seek sound medical advice, but pray for your doctor, that he or she may be guided by the Lord.

PRAYER. *Dear Lord, help me to receive the best care possible from my doctor.*

OME away with Me, by yourselves, to a deserted place and rest for a while.

—Mk 6:31

Take Care of Your Body As Well As Your Soul

REFLECTION. There is a direct link between the physical and the spiritual states of your being. You are one person, body and soul.

Take care of your soul, and your health will prosper. Prayer will help you to cope with the ups and downs of life.

PRAYER. *Lord, help me to treat my body as a tabernacle of Your Holy Spirit.*

ENCOURAGE one another and strengthen one another.

—1 Thes 5:11

MAY 12

Give a Pat on the Back to Someone Today

REFLECTION. Words of support can help heal a weary heart, and inspire perseverance in someone who is falling into despair.

Be a comfort to others when you see the need.

PRAYER. *Dear Jesus, I want to please You; help me to lift others up and not put them down.*

 YOU shall not bear any grudges against anyone, but you shall love your neighbor as yourself.

—Lev 19:18

MAY 13

Do Not Poison Your Mind with Hatred

REFLECTION. Resentment is very understandable. Some hurts run so deep that they are almost impossible to shrug off. But the one who suffers the most from a spirit of revenge is you.

Why carry such a needless burden?

PRAYER. *Dear Jesus, You forgave Your tormentors. Help me to forgive mine.*

E are regarded . . . as unknown men, and nevertheless we are well known; as dying, and behold we live on; as scourged, but we are not put to death; as sorrowful, and yet we are always rejoicing.

MAY 14

—2 Cor 6:8-10

Jesus Had to Suffer to Do God's Will

REFLECTION. We all have to bear crosses in this life. Trying to live a responsible and meaningful life won't be easy. It takes courage.

Once you understand that crosses are a normal part of life, it all becomes less difficult to manage.

PRAYER. *Dear Jesus, protect me from self-pity; help me to be courageous.*

E not afraid . . . because I am with you to deliver you.

MAY 15

—Jer 1:8

God Commands You Not to Be Afraid

REFLECTION. The road to mediocrity is paved with good intentions. Be a doer, not merely a hearer of the word of God.

Do not be afraid to act. God will bless you for your efforts to please Him.

PRAYER. *Holy Spirit, fill my soul with the confidence that I may please You in all I do.*

IVE thanks to the Lord, for He is good; **MAY**
His kindness endures forever.
—Ps 107:1 **16**

Open Your Eyes and See
the Goodness of the Lord

REFLECTION. You have been given everything: your body and soul, and life itself. Everything you have and everything you are comes from God.

Be still and drink this truth in: God is good.

PRAYER. *Give me a grateful heart, dear Lord, so I may appreciate Your gifts to the fullest.*

 UR citizenship is in heaven, and from **MAY**
there we await our Savior, the Lord
Jesus Christ. —Phil 3:20 **17**

Always Remember Your Final Destination

REFLECTION. Faith is having one foot on the ground and the other one in heaven.

God is your invisible companion through life. He is leading you to eternal joy.

PRAYER. *Help me, Lord, to remember that I belong to You.*

THIS is My beloved Son, in Whom I am well pleased.

—Mt 3:17

MAY 18

Be Assured of Your Privileged Position

REFLECTION. You are blessed and anointed. By Baptism you are a member of the Mystical Body of Christ.

The same favor that Jesus receives from His Father rests on you because you are His beloved child. Have confidence in His love.

PRAYER. *Dear Lord, thank You for making my life holy.*

THIS is my consolation in my distress: Your word gives me life.

—Ps 119:50

MAY 19

God Will Lift You Higher

REFLECTION. Just as a mother tends to the needs of her child, so does the Lord care for you. Trust in His love.

It's almost too good to be true, but the King of Kings loves you deeply.

PRAYER. *Dear Father in heaven, help me to abandon myself to Your love. In You I find my strength and joy.*

76

HEN you pray, go into your room, close the door, and pray to your Father in secret. —Mt 6:6

Prayer Is Raising Your Mind and Heart to God

REFLECTION. When it comes to pure prayer, the actual words you use do not matter as much as your desire to give yourself to God.

Silence is golden.

PRAYER. *Dear Jesus, You abandoned Yourself to the Father. Teach me how to do that.*

 HE Spirit Himself intercedes for us with sighs that cannot be put into words. —Rom 8:26

Wordless Prayer Is Called Contemplation

REFLECTION. The word "loneliness" tells us about the pain of being alone.

The word "contemplation" tells us about the glory of being alone with God.

PRAYER. *Dear Lord, some emotions are too deep to express in words. Please accept my silence as an act of love.*

AN any of you through worrying add a single moment to your span of life?
—Mt 6:27

Did You Know That
Your Sense of Humor Is From God?

REFLECTION. In life's dark moments, use your sense of humor to lighten the moment, and lift up your heart.

A little humor diffuses many a tense situation.

PRAYER. *Help me, Lord, to keep my sense of humor alive. May I always have a song in my heart.*

 N offended brother is stronger than a fortress, and quarrels are more difficult to overcome than castle gates.
—Prov 18:19

Quarreling Prevents Any Entry
into Your Heart

REFLECTION. Quarreling keeps people out of your love. It prevents love and peace from finding a resting place in your home.

A prayerful person can deal with a bickering relative because God supplies patience in difficult situations. Repeat the name of Jesus ten times, before you express your anger.

PRAYER. *Dear Lord, help me to remain calm in difficult family situations.*

F someone says, "I love God," but at the same time hates his brother, he is a liar.
—1 Jn 4:20

MAY 24

You Are a Good Person Trying to Be Better

REFLECTION. Don't be discouraged if you are not perfect. But try to cultivate a spirit of holy dissatisfaction with your meanness.

Turn it over to the Lord and pray for purification. He will cleanse you of all your faults.

PRAYER. *Dear Jesus, be my strength and my joy.*

 OLD fast to instruction and never let her go; guard her carefully, for she is your life.
—Prov 4:13

MAY 25

Be Wise and Listen to Those Who Love You

REFLECTION. Sometimes our parents and close friends see warning flags before we do. You may have to lead your own life, but the insights of others can protect you from making foolish mistakes in judgment.

Try to be more objective. Go for help.

PRAYER. *Lord, when a big decision is involved, help me to listen to good advice.*

OU lifted me up from the netherworld; You saved me from sinking into the pit. **MAY 26** —Ps 30:4

God Will Always Answer Your Pleas

REFLECTION. You don't have to hit bottom to come to your senses. The shock of losing control may serve as a wake-up call, but you will always have God at your side.

It's never too late to ask for help.

PRAYER. *Thank You, Father, for showing me how to pick up the pieces and carry on.*

 UT on the new self that is being renewed in the . . . image of its Creator. **MAY 27** —Col 3:10

Your Face Is the Face of Christ, Alive and Well

REFLECTION. St. Paul once said, "Now it is no longer I who live, but it is Christ Who lives in me" (Gal 2:20).

What would happen if today you pretended to be Jesus Christ? Without telling anyone what you were doing, how would you act? What kind of face would you show to the world?

PRAYER. *Jesus, teach me how to reveal Your goodness.*

HAT does it profit a man if he gains the whole world and loses or forfeits himself? —Lk 9:25 **MAY 28**

The Love of Money Is the Root of All Evil

REFLECTION. So many people struggle all through life to make more money, and if possible become a great success. But money doesn't buy happiness, and it surely doesn't get you into heaven.

Better for you if you rethink your priorities.

PRAYER. *Dearest Lord, teach me to measure my success according to Your Will.*

 HE Word of God is living and active [and] sharper than any two-edged sword. —Heb 4:12 **MAY 29**

The Bible Is Your Road Map to Heaven

REFLECTION. The good that you do will always follow you; so will the evil. There is a heaven, and there is a hell. Life is consequential.

When you read the Scriptures you are in touch with a road map to heaven.

PRAYER. *Dear Lord, help me to lift up my heart and have a new confidence that You will save me.*

IVE as children of light, for light produces all goodness and righteousness and truth.
—Eph 5:8-9

A Good Laugh Is Like Medicine for the Soul

REFLECTION. There is a wise saying that goes like this: "Jest for the health of it."

Laughter may not cure a cold, but it can lighten the burden of every single misery you'll ever have.

PRAYER. *Dear God, keep me from being needlessly dour. Help me to be a person of Your light and joy in the world.*

 , THE Lord, will hold your right hand. Do not be afraid. I will help you.
—Isa 41:13

Fear Is a Natural Reaction
to Perceived Danger

REFLECTION. Don't be afraid, because you are afraid. Fear is normal. We can never banish fear entirely, but we can refuse to become paralyzed by fear.

Turn your fears over right away, and imagine that the Lord is holding your right hand.

PRAYER. *Lord, let me feel Your touch this day.*

VERY good act of giving and every perfect gift are from above.

—Jas 1:17

JUNE 1

You Are Full of Wonder, Which Means Wonderful

REFLECTION. Every human being is essentially a magnificent creation. Relish this truth. You are destined to be totally free of pain and misery.

You have the power to bring to the world your own unique gifts and talents. Never underestimate what God can do with you.

PRAYER. *Lord of my life, make me an instrument of Your peace and love.*

 EFRESH yourselves with rich food and drink . . . for this day is holy unto the Lord . . . the joy of the Lord is your strength.

—Neh 8:10

JUNE 2

Be Positive and You Will Protect Your Health

REFLECTION. Victor Hugo once said, "Laughter is the sun that drives winter from the human face." It's easier to laugh when you develop a joyful attitude.

King David expressed his joy in these words, "I will bless the Lord at all times" (Ps 34:2).

PRAYER. *Lord, teach me how to cultivate a joyful attitude, so that Your praise may always be on my lips.*

WILL not allow any shameful act to be done before my eyes.

—Ps 101:3

JUNE 3

You Are the Observer of Your Thoughts

REFLECTION. You are not your thoughts. You are the guardian of your thoughts. St. Paul tells us to filter our thoughts.

Only think thoughts that are pure and of good report (Phil 4:8). Reject evil thoughts, and never put yourself down.

PRAYER. *Dear Lord, controlling my thoughts has been difficult for me. Help me to stay positive.*

 AM the way, and the truth, and the life. No one comes to the Father except through Me.

—Jn 14:6

JUNE 4

Jesus Will Do for You What
You Are Unable to Do for Yourself

REFLECTION. The Spirit of Jesus lives in all of His children. He enriches their lives with His wisdom and truth; and always leads them to His Holy Father.

Jesus is our indispensable guide to heaven.

PRAYER. *Dear Lord, show me the way to the Father. Increase in me the life of Your Holy Spirit.*

EFORE you were ever formed in your mother's womb, I saw you and approved you. —Jer 1:5

You and the Lord Go Way Back

REFLECTION. God knew you before you were born. He has given you certain gifts and talents to develop as you grow in His grace.

Feed His lambs with words of wisdom. Light the path for others and God will delight in you.

PRAYER. *Heavenly Father, help me to fulfill my potential. Give me the grace to overcome my selfishness.*

UT on the armor of God, so that you will be able to hold fast on the evil day. —Eph 6:13

You Are Not a Poor Helpless Creature

REFLECTION. There are times when we need a strong defense system against the attacks of the enemy.

Rely on the power of God's grace. He will shield you against your adversary.

PRAYER. *Dear Father, protect me against all the slings and arrows of life. Help me to stand fast in the tough times.*

THE Lord showers us with grace and glory. He does not withhold any good thing from those who walk in integrity.
—Ps 84:12

You Are God's Child

REFLECTION. The Lord favors you with His blessings. Think about all the good things God has given you: life, love, friends, family (how else could you have survived from infancy?). You are really blessed.

PRAYER. *Dear Lord, I am so grateful. I feel Your favor upon me. Help me to be a blessing to others.*

GLAD heart makes the face cheerful, but anguish of heart breaks one's spirit.
—Prov 15:13

You Are Not Your Thoughts

REFLECTION. You are the observer of your thoughts. You can reject negative thoughts, and you should or you will never rise above the image you have of yourself.

Aim high!

PRAYER. *Dear Lord, help me to take charge of my thoughts and cancel the ones that put me down.*

HERE there is envy and selfish ambition, there will also be disharmony and every type of wickedness. —Jas 3:16

Keeping the Peace Takes Moral Courage

REFLECTION. Words and actions can be abrasive and upsetting. Those who give in to their feelings can easily disturb the peace.

Those who practice self-restraint help to create an atmosphere of emotional comfort.

PRAYER. *Dear Father, give me the strength to hold my tongue when I want to scream in anger.*

 ROFESSING truth and love, we will in all things grow into Him Who is the head, Christ. —Eph 4:15

With God on Your Side
You Can Expect the Best

REFLECTION. We can do this because our hope is in the Lord. He is the best, and He gives the best.

The virtue of hope is defined as an expectation with confidence. God is on our side.

PRAYER. *Dear Lord, thank You for blessing me in the past and thank You for the blessings You plan for me in the future.*

FOR we are God's handiwork, created in Christ Jesus for a life of good works.
—Eph 2:10

Artists Love Their Created Works

REFLECTION. Keep in mind that God knew you before you were born.

God loves you, and has a plan for you. He made you to do a job in this world that nobody else can do.

PRAYER. *Dear Lord, deepen my awareness that I am an instrument of Your love.*

"**T**HEIR sins and their lawless acts I will remember no more." When these have been forgiven, there are no longer any offerings for sins. —Heb 10:17-18

Forgive, and You Will Be Forgiven

REFLECTION. God will forgive your sins and pay all your debts, but first He asks you to give amnesty to others who have offended you.

Mercy begets mercy. God is merciful, and He wants you to imitate Him.

PRAYER. *Holy Spirit, God of love, help me to save my soul, and to help save the souls of others.*

T IS You Who saved us from our enemies; You scattered in confusion those who hate us. —Ps 44:8

Enjoy the Victory Now That God Has Prepared for You in the Future

REFLECTION. Don't postpone joy. Even in joyless times, you can choose to be a joyful person. You can stand against the tide.

God will give you the victory, and you can anticipate His wonderful gifts.

PRAYER. *Heavenly Father, thank You for winning my victory over sin. Help me to realize that all the way to heaven is heaven.*

 EVER has the human heart imagined what God has prepared for those who love Him. —1 Cor 2:9

Heaven Is More Wonderful Than You Can Imagine

REFLECTION. All God asks is that you make a sensible effort to be good.

The rewards of virtue are visible on earth, but unimaginably spectacular in heaven. Hang in there.

PRAYER. *Dear God, help me to enjoy the wonders of the earth and to long for the wonders of eternity.*

HAVE come that they may have life, and have it in abundance.

—Jn 10:10

JUNE 15

Mental and Supernatural Health Should Be Your Primary Goal

REFLECTION. Human life is mortal. The body will dissolve into ashes. Everything around us will turn to dust.

But the life that Jesus gives will never end. It will carry you into eternity. Rejoice and be glad!

PRAYER. *Dear God, help me to anticipate the glory of heaven.*

 REJOICE when I endure weaknesses, insults, hardships, persecutions, and distress for the sake of Christ. For it is when I am weak that I am strong. —2 Cor 12:10

JUNE 16

Love Is Universal

REFLECTION. In some mysterious way, because we are intimately united with the heart of God; we are in touch with all the agony, pain, torture, and misery in the world.

PRAYER. *Dear Lord, You suffer with every one who suffers. Thank You for helping me to carry my cross.*

[ESUS] broke [the bread] and gave it to them, saying, "This is My Body, which will be given for you." —Lk 22:19

Christ's Death Is Re-presented at Every Catholic Mass

REFLECTION. The Holy Eucharist has provided strength and sustenance to Catholics for over two thousand years.

The Mass is a ritual, and a community prayer in which the one sacrifice on Calvary is re-presented on the altar.

PRAYER. *Lord, strengthen my faith in the Eucharist; feed me with the bread of Angels.*

 HEY forced me to look after the vineyards, but my own vineyard I could not watch over. —Song 1:6

Love Thyself

REFLECTION. Some people are good at taking care of everyone else, but not so good at taking care of themselves. See that this doesn't happen to you.

PRAYER. *God in heaven, I need wisdom to make the right choices in life. Give me the power to balance things in my favor once in a while.*

OR You are my refuge, a tower of strength against the enemy.

JUNE 19

—Ps 61:4

Trust the Lord

REFLECTION. Stand fast in your confidence. If you are armed with the armor of faith nothing can harm you.

You have real protection in the Lord, and this knowledge will give you peace of mind.

PRAYER. *Dear Lord, I will not be afraid, for You are always at my side.*

 HE Lord humbles and exalts . . . He raises the poor from the dust.

JUNE 20

—1 Sam 2:7-8

Be Brave, Take Heart!

REFLECTION. Nothing changes anxiety into joy like courage.

Courage conquers enemies from without and overcomes demons from within.

PRAYER. *Dear God, protect me from my own thoughts, and help me to be in the knowledge of Your Love.*

THE one who follows Me will never walk in darkness.

—Jn 8:12

Jesus Is the Light

REFLECTION. Jesus offers the brightest light, which can never be extinguished.

Choirs of Angels rejoice in His radiant presence. Follow Him.

PRAYER. *Heavenly Light, illuminate the path I need to travel. Guide me toward the light at the end of the tunnel.*

LET me worship Your Name with an undivided heart.

—Ps 86:11

Remain True to Your Word

REFLECTION. Honesty is like an icicle. Once it melts, that is the end of it.

Stand fast in your convictions.

PRAYER. *Dear Jesus, teach me to be true to my word, and true to You.*

HAVE told you these things so that My joy may be in you and your joy may be complete. —Jn 15:11 **JUNE 23**

A Smile Will Make Your Joy Visible

REFLECTION. Sometimes your joy can make you smile, but more often than not the decision to smile can be the source of your joy.

Choose joy, and smile more often.

PRAYER. *Dear Holy Spirit, remain in me, and help me to experience Your joy.*

 HERE the Spirit of the Lord is, there is freedom. —2 Cor 3:17 **JUNE 24**

You Are Free to Be Joyful

REFLECTION. Mother Teresa of Calcutta, now called Blessed Teresa, once said, "Joy is very infectious; therefore, be always full of joy. Joy can be your gift to the world."

PRAYER. *Lord, I want to rejoice in the knowledge of Your love. Please help me make that dream come true.*

BE diligent in providing a firm foundation for your call, . . . and you will receive a glorious welcome into the eternal kingdom.
—2 Pet 1:10-11

Salvation Is Yours for the Asking

REFLECTION. If you believe in God's love, you need not fear eternal judgment.

Lift up your heart, and live joyfully.

PRAYER. *Dear Lord, I am eternally grateful to You for the gift of life and the promise of heaven.*

JESUS stood up and cried out, "If anyone is thirsty, let him come to Me and drink."
—Jn 7:37

Jesus Will Quench Your Spiritual Thirst

REFLECTION. It happens every day; the Lord is continually filling your soul with the nectar of His Spirit. All you have to do is drink.

PRAYER. *Dear Jesus, thank You for satisfying my thirst.*

A Mature Christian Always Has a Happy Heart

REFLECTION. God created the most distant galaxy, and He created you.

That galaxy will turn to dust in time, but you will live forever.

PRAYER. *Dear Lord, I rejoice in the knowledge of Your love. Keep me humble, and help me to honor You all the days of my life.*

Pride Comes before the Fall

REFLECTION. God makes the rules. Don't fight Him.

The Church follows the words of Jesus; don't ridicule the Church.

PRAYER. *Dear Lord, help me to keep an attitude of humility. Tell me how I can help advance Your plan.*

I F a man makes a vow to the Lord, he shall not break his word.

—Num 30:3

The Letter of the Law Is Not Always Just

REFLECTION. Ideally vows are unconditionally binding. However, for the most part, vows are conditional promises. For example: "I will marry you for life, provided you don't beat me every day."

PRAYER. *Dear Lord, give me the wisdom to be non-judgmental and merciful in judging myself and others.*

W HERE there is wisdom there is strength, where there is strength there is understanding. —Bar 3:14

Wisdom Will Protect You from Being a Fool

REFLECTION. People are quick to believe idle rumors, false reports, and malicious gossip.

Rumors are not facts, and malicious gossip is the deliberate distortion of the truth. Don't be like the fool who rushes to judgment.

PRAYER. *Dear Lord, make me wise, slow to judge, and charitable in dealing with others.*

ET us love not in word or speech but in **JULY**
deed and truth.

—1 Jn 3:18 **1**

Actions Speak Louder Than Words

REFLECTION. Jesus told this parable: A father asked his son to do a chore. The son said he would, but he never did. Then he asked his second son to do it; that son said he would not, but later did it.

Then Jesus asked: which son obeyed his father? Deeds matter!

PRAYER. *Dear Father in heaven, give me the wisdom to say yes to Your Will, and the strength to carry out my noble desires.*

ELIVERANCE comes from the Lord. **JULY**
—Jon 2:10d **2**

God Will Supply All the Power

REFLECTION. The success of the 12-Step recovery program rests on the realization that each one of us is powerless.

Turning to God as the source of all power enables the addict to escape from the bondage of addiction.

PRAYER. *Dear God, You alone are my strength. Deliver me from every evil.*

HE kingdom of heaven is like a mustard seed.

—Mt 13:31

Your Tiniest Deed Pleases the Lord

REFLECTION. Mother Teresa, in helping the dying poor of Calcutta, once said: "What we are doing is just a drop in the ocean, but the ocean would be less because of that missing drop."

That is the attitude of a humble servant. Do what you can, and leave the rest to God.

PRAYER. *Help me, Jesus, to perform the duty of the present moment, however insignificant it may seem.*

 ITH the voice of thanksgiving, I will sacrifice to you.

—Jon 2:10ab

Thank You, God, for America the Beautiful

REFLECTION. "I recommend to all persons whomsoever, to observe July 4 as a day of public thanksgiving and prayer; to render their sincere and hearty thanks to the great Ruler of Nations for the manifold mercies, which distinguish our lot as a nation" (President George Washington, 1795).

PRAYER. *Dear God, thank You for the privilege of living in the United States of America.*

FALSE witness will not escape punishment, neither will the one who tells lies. —Prov 19:5

Honesty Is Its Own Reward

REFLECTION. An honest person is honored, while a liar is scorned. It's that simple.

Sooner or later, things will turn out badly for a liar. Decide to be honest, and enjoy your life more.

PRAYER. *Dear Lord, help me to tell the truth, and to be true to my word.*

 GOD has called us to holiness, not to impurity. —1 Thes 4:7

True Love Is a Choice

REFLECTION. Lust is the excessive preoccupation with sexual desires. Love is in the will to give yourself for the beloved. Say no to lust, and yes to love.

Love is patient; love is faithful; love is kind. Choose love.

PRAYER. *Lord, help me to love well. Keep my thoughts clean and my heart pure.*

WAITED patiently for the Lord; then He stooped down and heard my cry.

—Ps 40:2

Don't Give Up on God

REFLECTION. You may reach a point where you think God doesn't care about you anymore. Don't go down that road. God knows your heart, and He hears your cry.

Be patient with the Lord, and have confidence that He hears your cry for help.

PRAYER. *Heavenly Father, give me the strength to carry on. I place all my trust in You.*

 INCE we have such hope, we can act with complete confidence.

—2 Cor 3:12

Expect Good Things to Happen

REFLECTION. Hope is defined as an expectation with certainty. Sometimes it comes down to mind over matter. Keep your mind strong.

Expect the best. You won't regret it. God deserves your trust.

PRAYER. *Dear God, help me to act as if everything depended on me, and trust as if everything depended on You.*

HE Lord is in His holy temple; . . . His eyes are fixed on the world; His gaze examines everyone. —Ps 11:4

On Good Days and Bad, Keep the Faith

REFLECTION. Satchel Paige, the famous baseball pitcher once said, "Don't pray when it rains, if you don't pray when the sun shines."

That's good advice! Give praise to the Lord in all seasons.

PRAYER. *Heavenly Father, help me to praise Your Holy Name, especially when I least experience Your presence.*

OR where two or three are gathered together in My Name, I am there in their midst. —Mt 18:20

God Is Omnipresent

REFLECTION. God's presence penetrates and pervades every single atom. We are never alone. God permeates all of creation. When two or more come together, He is present among them.

Divine power is intensified by your awareness. Call on Him, and know that He will answer you.

PRAYER. *Dear Holy Spirit, in You we live and breathe. We praise You for Your glory.*

GOD is light, and there is no darkness at all in Him. . . . Live in the light.

—1 Jn 1:5, 7

Be Playful and Enjoy This Day

REFLECTION. "We don't stop playing because we get old; we get old because we stop playing" (another gem from Satchel Paige).

There is a kind of playfulness that comes from a grateful heart. Happiness is more attainable when you walk gratefully in the light.

PRAYER. *Lord, thank You for the gift of life and love. Give me a joyful, grateful heart in all circumstances.*

 DO not be afraid, do not be discouraged, for you will not suffer disgrace.

—Isa 54:4

Learn to Make Light of Your Fears

REFLECTION. Some fears are so deep that they come to us all the way from our childhood. We do not understand that these fears still have a certain power over us. But Jesus said, "Fear is useless; what you need is trust" (Lk 8:50). They can be overcome.

Focus more on God's love and less on your fears.

PRAYER. *Help me, Lord, to live joyfully because of the knowledge of Your love.*

O not worry about tomorrow. . . . Each day has enough troubles of its own.
—Mt 6:34

JULY 13

Live One Day at a Time

REFLECTION. Try not to tackle your whole life at once. Don't be a control-freak. Spare yourself the needless burden of worrying about something that may never happen.

Make this day a happy one.

PRAYER. *Dear Lord, take all my fears from me; help me to live in the present moment.*

HE Spirit Himself bears witness with our Spirit that we are children of God.
—Rom 8:16

JULY 14

What If Your Neighbor Was the Son of a King?

REFLECTION. Would you be extra nice and polite to that neighbor? Of course you would!

Now think of someone you dislike, and consider the fact that he or she is a child of the King of Kings.

PRAYER. *Dear Father, help me to show respect to all Your children, even the ones I dislike.*

E still and acknowledge that I am God. **JULY**
—Ps 46:11 **15**

The Only Language God Speaks Is Silence

REFLECTION. God's silence fills the universe.
You can hear God's wisdom in the silence of
your heart.

Be still, and rejoice in the knowledge of
God's silent presence.

PRAYER. *Lord, help me to know that You are
there comforting me.*

 F you wish to be perfect, . . . come, follow **JULY**
Me.
—Mt 19:21 **16**

A Spiritual Goal Will Give Your Life Purpose

REFLECTION. God has a job for you to do in this
world that nobody else can do. Fulfill your
spiritual goal, and you will find your joy.

God's Will for you is your destiny.

PRAYER. *Dear Lord, show me Your plan for my
life and help me to follow it.*

OUR hands have created and formed me; grant me understanding so that I may learn Your precepts. —Ps 119:73

The Conviction of God's Protection Will Save You Much Worry

REFLECTION. His will is going to triumph in the end, so you might as well relax and let God lead you.

All He asks is that you make a reasonable effort to be good.

PRAYER. *Lord, in You I find my strength and joy.*

 HE Lord is faithful. He will strengthen you and protect you from the evil one. —2 Thes 3:3

Never Let Yourself Be Separated from the Love of God

REFLECTION. In times of trouble, it is consoling to know that the Lord will never leave you.

If you invite Him to walk with you in this valley of tears, He will always be at your side.

PRAYER. *Dear Jesus, I know You are there for me; I fear no evil.*

Y soul shall greatly rejoice in the Lord.

—Isa 61:10

Live Your Life Joyfully

REFLECTION. As the earth brings forth her buds, so the Lord God will cause joy to flourish in your soul.

Joy is a gift, but it is one you must choose to accept in order to benefit from it.

PRAYER. *Bless me, Father, with a happy heart.*

ISTEN carefully to Me, says the Lord.

—Jer 17:24

Listen and You Will Learn

REFLECTION. Listening is an important part of loving. Make time to listen to those who need you.

Always show sincere interest in the words and feelings of the one speaking to you.

PRAYER. *Dear God, help me to love You by calmly listening to the person before me.*

I N Him we live and move and have our being. . . . We are all His offspring.
—Acts 17:28

God Is the Vine, of Which You Are a Branch.

REFLECTION. The vine carries its life to every branch. When a branch is broken off from the vine it loses its vitality and dies. It will never produce any fruit unless it is reattached.

Stay connected.

PRAYER. *Lord, I know that I am a part of You. Keep close to me forever.*

M AKE my joy complete by being of the same mind, having the same love for one another, and united in thought.
—Phil 2:2

You Never Have to Be Lonely

REFLECTION. People flock to those who are willing to listen. Become a good listener and you'll never be lonely again.

All it takes to break out of joyless isolation is a sympathetic ear.

PRAYER. *Help me, Lord, to be there for others.*

OU have turned my mourning into dancing.

—Ps 30:12a

JULY 23

God and Time Will Heal All Wounds

REFLECTION. Every sunrise is a new day, and a new beginning. Each day God gives us another opportunity to dance in the glow of His light and happiness.

Don't stand there watching; join the dance.

PRAYER. *O Lord, I dance in Your Holy Presence. My heart sings for joy.*

HE grace of God has appeared bringing salvation to the entire human race.

—Tit 2:11

JULY 24

God's Amazing Grace Will Save You

REFLECTION. John Newton was an 18th century despised slave trader, whose conversion to Christ changed him into an anti-slavery activist. As a result he wrote the song, "Amazing Grace."

He said, "If Grace can change a wretch like me, it can change you too."

PRAYER. *Work a miracle in my life, O Lord; deliver me from my worst weakness.*

MAY the God of hope fill you with all joy and peace in believing, so that you may grow rich in hope by the power of the Holy Spirit.

JULY 25

—Rom 15:13

If You Are Happy, Please Notify Your Face

REFLECTION. Be happy within yourself so that you can be happy with those around you.

The ultimate goal is to be happy with God for all eternity.

PRAYER. *Dear God, help me to be a sign of Your love and joy to others.*

———————

GOD is love, and whoever abides in love abides in God, and God in him.

JULY 26

—1 Jn 4:16

Even at Midnight the Sun is Still Shining

REFLECTION. Whether you feel the sun or not doesn't matter, it is still shining.

The same is true for God. His love is always present, whether you feel it or not.

PRAYER. *Dear Lord, help me to trust Your love no matter what.*

BE reconciled with your brother. Come to terms quickly with your opponent.

—Mt 5:23, 25

JULY
27

Forgiveness Is Good for Your Health

REFLECTION. It never hurts to break the ice when hurt feelings are involved. Why not just call to say you're sorry if you are in any way at fault?

Decide to forgive, if you have been hurt in any way. Begin the process of healing, for peace of soul to return.

PRAYER. *Lord, help me to forgive before I feel like it.*

THE measure that you use for others will be used to measure you.

—Mt 7:2

**JULY
28**

God Loves a Cheerful Giver

REFLECTION. Kindness begets kindness. If you want to receive love, then give love.

Give without counting the cost. What you give to others will come back to you.

PRAYER. *Heavenly Father, help me to be a generous giver.*

ORD, You are the potter, we are the work of Your hands.

—Isa 64:7

Your Life Is a Work in Process

REFLECTION. If you feel useless, discouraged, or ugly today, remember this:

"Just when the caterpillar thought her life was over, she became a butterfly."

PRAYER. *Lord, keep my faith alive, especially when I'm blue. Your wonderful promises give me hope.*

———————

OU must regard yourselves as being dead to sin and alive for God in Christ Jesus.

—Rom 6:11

Don't Let the Past Drag You Down

REFLECTION. Over a million shoplifters are arrested in America every year. If you have ever shoplifted, and gotten away with it, you owe society a debt.

Why not write a check to your favorite charity in reparation for all your sins?

PRAYER. *Dear Jesus, help me to forgive myself for my many follies.*

SE whatever gift each one of you has received to serve one another.

—1 Pet 4:10

Be a Good Steward of All Your Gifts

REFLECTION. No matter how modest your means, you can always find a way to help someone in need.

A kind word, an unexpected phone call, or a few dollars given in a time of need can soothe an aching heart.

PRAYER. *Jesus, my Savior, increase my desire to be a good steward of my time and talents.*

 OUR statutes . . . are the very joy of my heart.

—Ps 119:111

The Joys of Life Are a Blessing

REFLECTION. The joys of life take many forms; seeing the awesome beauty of nature, feeling the freshness of a spring rain, listening to the laughter of children.

Joy stays with you and nourishes your soul.

PRAYER. *Dear Lord, Your presence in my life is a joy forever.*

PEN your mouth wide so that I may fill it. . . . If only My people would listen to Me. —Ps 81:11, 14

AUG. 2

Expect God to Feed You

REFLECTION. Be simple and hopeful like a baby bird awaiting its mother's return.

God takes care of those whom He loves. He brings the grace you need each day, but you must open your soul to receive it.

PRAYER. *Lord, I stand ready, willing, and able to let You feed me this day.*

 E cast out the spirits with a command and cured all who were sick. —Mt 8:16

AUG. 3

Jesus Will Heal You Too

REFLECTION. Even if you are frightened, and slow to recover, maintain your trust in the Lord's power. Put your fate in His care.

Faith is as important to recovery as good medicine.

PRAYER. *Lord, You are my Divine Physician. In You I place my trust.*

THE mind of one who is wise seeks further knowledge. . . . Plans miscarry when counsel is lacking, but they succeed when there are many counselors.

—Prov 15:14, 22

Look before You Leap

REFLECTION. Get help: ask directions. Be clear about your goals. Otherwise you may get lost in the fray.

So plan ahead, ask for advice, pray, and be at peace.

PRAYER. *Give me good advisors, Lord, and help me to listen to them.*

LIVE in a manner worthy of the Lord and become fully pleasing to Him.

—Col 1:10

First of All, Get Enough Sleep

REFLECTION. Are you sleep deprived? You can't be strong or forceful if you are a walking zombie.

To do your best take better care of yourself. Get the sound sleep you need.

PRAYER. *Help me, Lord, to get my needed rest, for my own good, and for the good of those around me.*

OU would do well to pay close attention . . . until the day dawns and the morning star rises in your hearts.
—2 Pet 1:19

**AUG.
6**

Today We Celebrate the Transfiguration

REFLECTION. Jesus became the light of the world in a visible way. He wants you to become a light to others as well.

You are like a letter from Him to the world; a letter written not with ink, but with the spirit of the living God.

PRAYER. *Dear Jesus, make me an instrument of Your love.*

 LWAYS be sober. Endure hardships, do the work of preaching the Gospel, and carry out your ministry to the fullest extent.
—2 Tim 4:5

**AUG.
7**

If at First You Don't Succeed, Try, Try Again

REFLECTION. A book by Laurence J. Peter, a Canadian psychologist, entitled *The Peter Principle,* was rejected by 30 publishers before the William Morrow Company gave it a chance. It went on to sell over 200,000 copies in the first year, and made a small fortune for its author who never gave up trying.

PRAYER. *Jesus, grant me the grace to persevere, especially when it comes to doing Your Will.*

116

GOD created man in His own image, in the divine image He created him; male and female He created them.

—Gen 1:27

AUG. 8

Each Person Reflects God's Being in a Unique Way

REFLECTION. Grass is grass; or is it that simple? Bamboo belongs to the grass family, but in China it is used as scaffolding in the building of skyscrapers. Grass isn't always as weak as you think.

What outstanding quality has God given you?

PRAYER. *Lord, let me know my strengths so that I may use them in serving You.*

HOEVER can be trusted in small matters can also be trusted in great ones.

—Lk 16:10

AUG. 9

Fidelity to the Duty of the Present Moment

REFLECTION. Remember the song "Little Things Mean a Lot?" It is true.

If everybody did the few simple things they know they ought to do, the big problems would take care of themselves.

PRAYER. *God Almighty, You gave me gifts and talents; help me to use them well.*

AIT quietly for the Lord and be patient until He comes. Do not fret over the man who prospers.

AUG.
10

—Ps 37:7

Envy Is Sadness over the Good Fortune of Another

REFLECTION. Envy will condemn you to perpetual sadness. Why be envious? Try not to think about those who are better off than you.

Leave the justice issue to God, and be happy.

PRAYER. *Lord, don't let me give in to envy. Help me to have a cheerful heart.*

 EAL with others as you would like them to deal with you.

AUG.
11

—Mt 7:12

Do Something Nice for Someone Today

REFLECTION. Give someone a compliment, offer some practical help to a neighbor, or give a small child a coin and a smile.

Do it as a sign of your loving heart.

PRAYER. *Help me, Lord, to make small gestures of love.*

UR own conscience is clear, and our desire is to act honorably in everything we do. —Heb 13:18

AUG.
12

Stand Up for the Truth

REFLECTION. If something hits you the wrong way, express your opinion. Don't be afraid to say, "This is wrong and I won't stand for it."

People will never forget your courage.

PRAYER. *Holy Spirit, give me the courage I need to be a faithful witness to the truth.*

 RIDE goes before disaster, and a haughty spirit goes before a fall. —Prov 16:18

AUG.
13

Self-Confidence Is Not Pride

REFLECTION. Pride is an inordinate love of self. A proud person puts other people down, whereas a self-confident person is humble as he proudly raises them up.

In using your talents for others, you show your kindness and love.

PRAYER. *Father, You are the giver of all gifts. I bow humbly before You and pray for the grace to serve You well.*

119

D O not forget to offer hospitality to strangers, for by doing this some have entertained Angels without knowing it. —Heb 13:2

America Has Always Welcomed Strangers

REFLECTION. Over 100 million Americans are the descendants of 17 million immigrants who were processed through Ellis Island in New York harbor.

All of these strangers came to our shores with high hopes of making a better life. We are the descendants of immigrants.

PRAYER. *Dear Jesus, give me the eyes of faith to see You in every stranger.*

A LL wisdom derives from the Lord and remains with Him forever. —Sir 1:1

Go and "Do Whatever He Tells You."

REFLECTION. On this the Feast of the Assumption of Mary into Heaven, we celebrate her final victory over this valley of tears.

We honor her because by her life she taught us this one great truth, "Do whatever He tells you."

PRAYER. *Hail Mary, full of grace, the Lord is with you.*

THE violence of the wicked will sweep them away because they refuse to do what is right. —Prov 21:7

The Terrorists Are Deadly Bullies

REFLECTION. Whatever their ideological convictions, Muslim extremists have turned against the will of Allah.

They call evil good, and good evil. In the end they will perish.

PRAYER. *Lord, help me not to be afraid of demonic power. May the good Muslims prevail over the extremists.*

TO each of us, the manifestation of the Spirit is given for the common good. —1 Cor 12:7

A Garden Is Beautiful Because of Its Variety

REFLECTION. Every individual contributes something unique to make this a more wonderful world. Every gift and talent counts, like the flowers in a garden.

God delights in your unique contribution to advance the common good.

PRAYER. *Help me, Lord, to value and celebrate my gifts.*

THE righteous are as confident as young lions.

—Prov 28:1

AUG.
18

Male Lions Are Overrated

REFLECTION. Lions are felines, and they like to nap all day. The males let the females do all the hunting, and then push everyone aside, demanding to eat first.

If you really want to be righteous you'd be better off imitating poodles. They bark fearlessly at elephants.

PRAYER. *Jesus, give me the courage to challenge the powerful when they are wrong.*

 FLOOD waters cannot quench love, nor can torrents drown it.

—Song 8:7

AUG.
19

True Love Is Unselfish

REFLECTION. Those who truly love one another are ready to give up their lives for their beloved.

Romantic love is often self-serving, but true love puts the beloved first.

PRAYER. *Jesus, You showed Your love for us on the Cross. Give me a loving heart like Yours.*

GIVE thanks to the Lord on the harp; offer praise to Him on the ten-stringed lyre. —Ps 33:2

A Joyful Heart Is a Ten-Stringed Lyre

REFLECTION. You praise the Lord day and night when you remain gratefully aware of His endless love for you.

The heart sings its praises in the silence of a smile.

PRAYER. *You, Lord, are awesome; what more can I say? Thank You for caring for me.*

MY steadfast love shall not depart from you. —Isa 54:10

AUG. 21

Keep Working on Your Dreams

REFLECTION. Dreams are the seeds of great deeds.

Because God is the source of all our good thoughts and dreams, presume that He will bring to fruition all that He inspires in you.

PRAYER. *Inspire me, Lord, with dreams that give me hope.*

OU are to go and proclaim the **Kingdom of God.**

—Lk 9:60

Keep Your Sights Set on the Lord

REFLECTION. If you have any hope of persevering in your good intentions you are going to need the grace of God.

Be smart. Look to Jesus day in and day out, and ask for His grace.

PRAYER. *Dear Jesus, keep my eyes fixed on You and my heart filled with Your love for others.*

EEK His Kingdom, and these things will be given to you as well.

—Lk 12:31

Think of Life As a Test

REFLECTION. Some think the Christian life is a trial. Why not think of it as an easy test?

It is a time for tending to yourself, a time of training for the race, a time of preparation.

PRAYER. *Dear Jesus, help me to seek Your Kingdom above all else.*

HE Lord is in His sacred temple; silence before Him, all the earth.

—Hab 2:20

AUG. 24

The Church Is a Sacred Place

REFLECTION. Step out of the world every once in a while. Enter the silence of your local church. Smell the candles, and rest before the Lord in the tabernacle.

Be still and know that He is God.

PRAYER. *Dear Jesus, deepen my sense of reverence for the Holy Eucharist.*

E would feed [you] with the finest of wheat and . . . honey from the rock.

—Ps 81:17

AUG. 25

The Eucharist Is God-with-Us

REFLECTION. No one can describe the indescribable. The word ineffable refers to profound mystery.

We know that Jesus is present in the Eucharist, but we can't explain how. It doesn't matter. Enjoy the mystery.

PRAYER. *Dear God, thank You for coming to us and for blessing us with Your presence.*

AVE mercy on me, O God, in accord with Your kindness.

—Ps 51:3

God Is Attracted to the Humble

REFLECTION. The Book of Psalms is a spiritual treasure.

Jesus told a parable about a tax collector who stood off at a distance and prayed, "God, be merciful to me, a sinner" (Lk 18:13). Jesus praised him for his humility, and the tax collector "returned to his home justified" (Lk 18:14).

PRAYER. *Dear Lord, give me a humble heart, that I may win Your blessing.*

 N honorable name is more to be desired than great riches.

—Prov 22:1

Your Reputation Is Your Legacy

REFLECTION. Being a crowd pleaser is no way to build a good reputation. But standing up for the truth against public opinion is.

Stay focused and do the right thing.

PRAYER. *Lord, I want to do Your Will. I leave my reputation to the history books.*

PRAISE the Lord, O Jerusalem! For He . . . blesses your children within you.

—Ps 147:12-13

AUG.
28

The Blessings of God Give Us Joy

REFLECTION. St. Augustine said, "We are an Easter People, and Alleluia is our song."

When the going gets rough, think of God's constant blessings. This eternal truth will lift your drooping spirit. It is all in the mind.

PRAYER. *Jesus, teach me how to control my thoughts with the truth of our faith. Help me to reject fear.*

DO not fear, for I have redeemed you; I have called you by name; you are Mine.

—Isa 43:1

AUG.
29

If God Is for You, Who Can Be against You?

REFLECTION. Don't let yourself believe that you are a poor helpless creature, alone against the world. Not so!

The Lord claims you as His own; He will not let you go.

PRAYER. *Heavenly Father, I am under the shadow of Your wings; You alone give me peace.*

127

FOR you have been my fortress, my refuge in times of trouble.

—Ps 59:17

**AUG.
30**

God Protects You from Self-Sabotage

REFLECTION. Which is your real enemy? Is it Satan, or are your own sins your greatest enemy?

Be aware of the opponent within, and ask God to protect you from your own inordinate desires.

PRAYER. *Lord, cleanse me of my sins and shield me from temptation.*

 LOVE your enemies and pray for those who persecute you. This will make you children of your heavenly Father.

—Mt 5:44-45

**AUG.
31**

Do Not Allow Hatred to Take Root in You

REFLECTION. Hatred is the enemy of happiness. Avoid as much as possible anyone who persecutes you, but do not descend into hatred.

Jesus said, "I have told you these things so that . . . your joy may be complete" (Jn 15:11).

PRAYER. *Lord of life, bless me with the strength to at least strive for the impossible, namely to love my enemy.*

GOD, hear my cry and listen to my prayer. . . . I will abide in Your tent forever and find refuge in the shelter of Your wings. —Ps 61:2, 5

SEPT.

1

God Will Come to Your Rescue

REFLECTION. Do not lose hope believing that God's silence is a sign that He has abandoned you.

The Psalm continues, "For You, O God, have heard my vows and granted me the heritage of those who fear Your Name" (Ps 61:6).

PRAYER. *Divine Lord, I plead for Your help, and I believe You will hear and answer me.*

WILL bless You all my life; with uplifted hands I will call on Your name.

—Ps 63:5-6

SEPT.

2

Whoever Rejoices in God Wins His Favor

REFLECTION. The Scriptures tell us three things about God: God is powerful; God is kind; and God rewards "each person in accordance with his deeds" (Ps 62:13).

Lift up your heart and have a new confidence, and remember charity overcomes a multitude of sins.

PRAYER. *Father in heaven, make me a prayerful person. Teach me to rejoice in the knowledge of Your love.*

TOO heavy for us are our sins, and only You can blot them out.

—Ps 65:4

Deliverance Is Sweeter Than Riches

REFLECTION. The Lord comes to set His people free, and bring them to the promised land. Delivering us from our slavery to sin, He sets us on the path to heaven.

Be grateful that you have the wisdom to understand the stakes.

PRAYER. *Lord, let Your face of love shine upon me that I may live forever in Your light.*

MAKE haste, O God, to rescue me; O Lord, come quickly to my aid.

—Ps 70:2

When the Flood-Waters Reach Your Neck, You Are Still Safe

REFLECTION. The Psalmist is in great distress, pleading with God to intervene. Have you ever known such desperation? This Psalm ends on a positive note, "You are my help and my deliverer" (Ps 70:6).

Have confidence, because in your hour of need God will be with you.

PRAYER. *Dear Lord, I believe. Help me in my unbelief.*

FROM the time you were a child you have known the sacred Scriptures. From these you can acquire the wisdom that will lead you to salvation. —2 Tim 3:15

Read the Bible to Learn God's Will for You

REFLECTION. A woman saw her doctor reading the Bible one day. She asked, "Does reading the Scriptures help you before you perform the surgery, or after?" He answered softly, "During."

Prepare your mind for the task ahead by finding out how God thinks.

PRAYER. *Father in heaven, give me an attitude of humble obedience to Your word, that I may do Your Will.*

 ALL Scripture is inspired by God and is useful for teaching, for refutation, for correction, and for training in uprightness. —2 Tim 3:16

God Speaks to Us in the Bible

REFLECTION. God's word comes to us in revelation. The Bible teaches us the truths we need to know in order to attain salvation.

Life is a long drive in the wilderness, and the Bible is our companion, and at times our road map.

PRAYER. *Keep me on the right path, O Lord. I yearn to see Your face.*

ESUS performed many other signs . . . that are not recorded in this work. But those written here have been recorded so that you may come to believe. —Jn 20:30-31

Tradition Preceded the Written Word

REFLECTION. The Gospels are the written accounts of the early preaching of the Apostles.

The Apostles told others about the Lord's words and deeds hoping to convert them to have faith in Him. Since then billions of people have come to know Him.

PRAYER. *Lord God, thank You for bringing me the Good News of the Gospel.*

 LESSED is the womb that bore You and the breasts that nursed You! —Lk 11:27

Hail Mary, Full of Grace

REFLECTION. This day is Mary's birthday, and mine. I have always been aware of her two-fold vocation: 1) to bring Jesus into the world, and 2) to give Him back to the world. This is my vocation and yours as well.

We bring Jesus into the world when we accept Him in our hearts, and we give Him back to the world when we love one another.

PRAYER. *Lord, help me to be a carrier of Your divine love.*

JESUS responded, . . . "I am not alone because the Father is with Me." —Jn 16:31-32

On the Cross Jesus Said,
"My God, My God, Why Have You
Forsaken Me?" (Mk 15:34)

REFLECTION. Both statements are true because Jesus was both human and divine. As humans we, too, know about those dark feelings that sometimes beset us. And yet there is always hope.

Because of God's grace we know we are never alone.

PRAYER. *Lord, help me not to be afraid. I know You are always with me.*

 WHEN I am terrified, I place my trust in You. . . . In God, I place my trust and know no fear. —Ps 56:4, 5

The Lord Sustains You in Your Hour of Need

REFLECTION. Write down all your troubles. Then crumble that piece of paper and hold it in the palm of your hand. Now, make a decision to live your life joyfully, in spite of all the worries.

God will be there to sustain you in that good intention.

PRAYER. *Lord, I trust in You especially when I feel overwhelmed.*

GOD, be gracious to us and bless us and let Your face shine upon us.

—Ps 67:2

God's Face Shines Upon You

REFLECTION. In Hebrew, God's face shining upon a person means that he is smiling and approving of you. When a "face shines" it is an idiom for a smile.

What a lovely thought. God is smiling at you right now.

PRAYER. *Dear Lord, how grateful I am for Your gracious smile.*

HEN you cried out to Me in distress, I rescued you.

—Ps 81:8

God Has Great Things in Store for You

REFLECTION. The Lord freed His people from slavery. He blessed them with manna in the desert.

"Why are you so frightened, O you of little faith?" (Mt 8:26).

PRAYER. *Jesus, rescue me from my doubts and fears; help me to live joyfully.*

HY, O God, have you cast us off forever? Why does Your anger blaze forth against the sheep of Your pasture? —Ps 74:1

It's Human to Be Perplexed

REFLECTION. The mystery of God's silence, when tragedy strikes, is terribly disturbing for everyone. But take heart, Jesus has come to establish justice.

Give Him time, and you will understand. All will be well.

PRAYER. *Dear Jesus, on the Cross You asked "Why?" I know I am not greater than You. Teach me to accept my perplexity graciously.*

 E will have pity on the lowly and the poor; the lives of the needy He will save. —Ps 72:13

The Poor in Spirit Attract God's Mercy

REFLECTION. The poor are usually those who are lowly, oppressed, and without power. You may not be materially poor, but are you in need of God's strength for any reason?

As soon as you tell Him about it, the Lord God is at your side. Things will get better immediately.

PRAYER. *Father, into Your hands I commend my spirit.*

135

LORD, You are kind and forgiving, filled with kindness for all who cry to You. —Ps 86:5

Don't Let the Past Drag You Down

REFLECTION. Did you know that 75% of the people who go for psychotherapy do it because of guilt feelings?

To offset guilt, remember that God is nothing but mercy and forgiveness.

PRAYER. *Dear Lord, I know You forgive me; help me to forgive myself.*

 OD raised this Jesus to life. Of that we are all witnesses. —Acts 2:32

Christ is Resurrected in Me

REFLECTION. Remember the words of St. Paul, "I live, no not I, but Christ lives in me." That idea is literally true.

The transforming power of Jesus Christ is active in you right now. Accept and celebrate the glory that is in you.

PRAYER. *Father, let me feel the power of Jesus living in my mind, body, and spirit.*

F God is for us, who can be against us? He did not spare His own Son but gave Him up for all of us. —Rom 8:31

 F God is for us, who can be against us? He did not spare His own Son but gave Him up for all of us. —Rom 8:31

SEPT.
17

God Wants You to Succeed

REFLECTION. There are many mechanical parts to a seafaring ship. Alone, all of them would sink immediately, but when they are in their proper place the ship floats.

So it is with you. Your dark side could sink you in a second. Fortunately, the Lord has arranged everything so that your grace-filled soul will float up to heaven.

PRAYER. *Dear Lord, I put my hope in You.*

 LACE your hope in the Lord: be strong and courageous in your heart, and place your hope in the Lord. —Ps 27:14

SEPT.
18

God Keeps His Promises—Be Patient

REFLECTION. God has promised strength to make up for your weakness, and light to lead you in those times of darkness.

Grace from above is there for the asking. Why do you worry so?

PRAYER. *Lord, I need to be more trusting. You are always with me, but sometimes I forget. Increase my trust.*

137

HE Lord is my shepherd; there is nothing I shall lack. He makes me lie down in green pastures; He leads me to tranquil streams. —Ps 23:1-2

The Lord Will Comfort You

REFLECTION. Even though you walk through the valley of darkness, do not fear any evil for the Lord is with you to comfort you.

Open yourself to the God of all consolation.

PRAYER. *Jesus, You are the Good Shepherd. Help me to remember that You are near.*

 UR Father in heaven, hallowed be Your Name. —Mt 6:9

The Liturgy Enables You to Worship Wisely

REFLECTION. Jesus never taught us to say, "My Father Who art in heaven. . ." He called us to worship as a people, in a faith community.

Once a week, at least, remember to keep holy the Sabbath day by attending Holy Mass, if your health permits.

PRAYER. *Dear Lord, give me the grace to attend Mass regularly.*

COME, let us sing with jubilation to the Lord; let us cry out to the Rock of our salvation. —Ps 95:1

Let Your Joy Be Made Audible

REFLECTION. Even when you are discouraged, remember that you owe God a debt of gratitude for all that he has done for you.

Think more about God's love, and less about your troubles and woes.

PRAYER. *Jesus, my heart overflows with joyful praise. Help me to smile more.*

LET your minds be filled with whatever is true, whatever is honorable, whatever is just, whatever is pure. —Phil 4:8

Keep Your Mind Clean

REFLECTION. Whether you are now in a state of sickness, perplexity, imprisonment, or depression, you can still be content within if you learn to control your thoughts.

PRAYER. *Dear Lord, help me to cancel negative thinking and stay positive.*

W E are afflicted on all sides but not crushed, bewildered but not sunk in despair. —2 Cor 4:8

SEPT. 23

Do Not Lose Heart

REFLECTION. God knows your feelings. It pleases Him when you do not let your feelings run away with you.

Be confident. Feelings are not facts.

PRAYER. *God, grant me the strength to face each day with renewed courage.*

M Y help comes from the Lord, the Maker of heaven and earth. —Ps 121:2

SEPT. 24

You Are Always in God's Care

REFLECTION. God will not let your foot slip; He will protect you from all evil, and look after your coming in and going out.

Believe this, and you will have a good frame of mind, which in turn will keep you content.

PRAYER. *Dear Lord, I rest in the security of Your loving care.*

ONE of us lives for himself, and none of us dies for himself.

—Rom 14:7

You Will Not Die Alone

REFLECTION. Death comes to everyone sooner or later, and we must be ready; but in the meantime, do not fret needlessly.

When the time comes, God will be with you, and He will put your fears to rest.

PRAYER. *Dear Father, comfort me in the hour of my death. Bring me safely home and give me peace.*

OR God so loved the world that He gave His only Son, so that everyone who believes in Him may not perish. —Jn 3:16

God Wills That You Be Saved

REFLECTION. That's the good news. The bad news is that at times you may not feel like you're being saved.

Pay no attention to your feelings. Give yourself to God, and trust in Him.

PRAYER. *Father in heaven, bring me home to You.*

HE fruit of the Spirit is love, joy, peace, patience, kindness, generosity, faithfulness, gentleness, and self-control.
—Gal 5:22-23

SEPT. 27

A Good Tree Produces Good Fruit

REFLECTION. Never be discouraged simply because you're not perfect.

When you examine your conscience look and see all the love and peace and joy and goodness that has come out of your soul over the years, and perk up.

PRAYER. *Holy Spirit, I'm far from holy, but by Your grace I have tried to be kind and loving, most of the time. Thank You for Your presence in my life.*

———

HE Lord is near. Do not worry about anything. . . . Then the peace of God, . . . will guard your hearts and your minds in Christ Jesus.   —Phil 4:5, 7

SEPT. 28

God Will Hear Your Pleas

REFLECTION. Why not put on the will to be peaceful? You are not in danger.

The peace of God goes beyond all understanding. He will comfort you.

PRAYER. *Holy Lord, Your peace is my strength.*

HE grace of the Lord Jesus Christ and the love of God and the fellowship of the Holy Spirit be with you all.

SEPT. 29

—2 Cor 13:13

God Is Blessing You This Day

If you pray for God to bless you, or anyone else, be assured that He will, because it is His nature to bless everyone who wants His blessing. However, He likes to hear you ask for His blessing.

PRAYER. Lord God, may I have the favor of Your blessing this day and every day.

———————

 AY they also be in us so that the world may believe that You have sent Me.

SEPT. 30

—Jn 17:21

Jesus Came to Claim You

REFLECTION. A native African explained the way his people think of God. He said, "We don't have to search for God, He searches for us. God is like a lion hunting for good. We are His prey. Once He charges and seizes us, the chase is over."

PRAYER. Dear Lord, You are the hunter, and I surrender to You.

143

F you remain faithful to My word, . . . you will know the truth, and the truth will set you free. —Jn 8:31-32

OCT.
1

You and God Have the Same Goal, Heaven

REFLECTION. God wants you to find eternal happiness. Isn't that what you want too? Then why do you ever allow yourself to think that God is distant?

He always cares; it is you who lose trust.

PRAYER. *Dear Jesus, You have taught us that You are Love. I never want to forget that.*

 E will command His Angels about you—to guard you wherever you go. —Ps 91:11

OCT.
2

The Angels Are Here to Help You

REFLECTION. This is the feast of the Guardian Angels. The most important thing to remember today is that there are superior beings helping you. They are invisible, but ever attentive to your needs.

You can send your Angel to help someone you love at anytime.

PRAYER. *Dear Jesus, keep me aware of my Guardian Angel. I need all the help I can get.*

144

DESPITE all of our afflictions, I am greatly encouraged and overflowing with joy. —2 Cor 7:4

OCT. 3

Cheer Up, for the Lord's Joy Is in You

REFLECTION. St. Paul encouraged us to rejoice in all circumstances. He wrote those words while he was in prison. If he can find joy in the midst of such misery, so can you.

Take heart and find the Spirit of Joy residing in you.

PRAYER. *Holy Spirit, soul of my soul, lift me up beyond my woes and give me joy.*

[**J**ESUS] said, "Follow Me. . . . No one who puts his hand to the plow and then looks back is fit for the Kingdom of God." —Lk 9:59, 62

OCT. 4

Leave Everything and Follow the Lord

REFLECTION. St. Francis of Assisi left his family behind. His father wanted him to take over the family business, but he answered a higher calling. He said, "First things first." He gave God the best he had.

PRAYER. *Dear Lord, I give You my life. Show me how to live it well for You.*

HE harvest is abundant, but the laborers are few. Therefore, ask the Lord of the harvest to send forth laborers for His harvest.
—Lk 10:2

OCT. 5

Every Person Has a Duty to Try to Save Souls

REFLECTION. Are you aware of how important this is? Jesus said, "Do you love me? . . . Feed My lambs . . . Feed My sheep" (Jn 21:15-17).

What are you doing to answer that challenge?

PRAYER. *Dear Jesus, help me to love You more, by working to save others.*

 HOEVER listens to you listens to Me, and whoever rejects you rejects Me.
—Lk 10:16

OCT. 6

Affirm the Body of Christ

REFLECTION. The Church is the Mystical Body of Christ. To hear the Vicar of Christ is to hear Christ Himself.

Affirm the divine element, and support the human element as best you can.

PRAYER. *Heavenly Father, give me the humility to submit to the authority of the Church.*

OMAN, you have great faith. Let it be done for you as you wish.

—Mt 15:28

The Holy Rosary Is about the Life of Christ

REFLECTION. Faith is like a tiny flame. It needs to be guarded from outside forces.

Praying the rosary helps us to keep our minds attentive to the truths of our faith, as we focus on the mysteries of the life of Jesus and His Mother.

PRAYER. *Jesus, Your life is an inspiration to me. Deepen my love for You.*

N the world you will endure suffering. But take courage! I have overcome the world.

—Jn 16:33

Jesus Will Guide You

REFLECTION. The promises of God open the doors of hope and joy for us. Despair and doubt close them.

Stay close to Jesus, and trust Him. Spiritual progress takes time; be patient.

PRAYER. *Dear Lord, teach me to hope for the best and to seek Your guidance.*

HATEVER you did for one of the least of these brethren of Mine, you did for Me. —Mt 25:40

OCT. 9

Jesus Comes to Us in Distressing Disguises

REFLECTION. The fat lady is Christ. The dirty hobo is Christ. The beautiful child is Christ. The priest is Christ.

Treat everyone with the respect they deserve because they carry the Lord with them; sometimes in distressing disguises, sometimes not.

PRAYER. *Dear Jesus, give me the eyes to see You in the least of my neighbors.*

OU will forget your wretchedness, remembering it only as floodwaters gone by. —Job 11:16

OCT. 10

Time Heals All Wounds

REFLECTION. Let go of your hurtful memories. Try not to think about those unhappy times.

Gradually you will forget the pain, you will forgive, and your heart will be healed.

PRAYER. *Father, do not let me dwell on past hurts; heal me in the depths of my soul.*

B E brave and steadfast and without fear. . . . It is the Son of God Who goes with you.
—Deut 31:6

If You Let Him, God Will Plan Your Day

REFLECTION. Let the plan of God unfold in your life. Give it time to develop and stay calm under the shadow of His wings.

God actually plans your life, right down to the hour.

PRAYER. *Lord, let my perplexity serve You; deliver me from fear.*

B LESSED are you when people insult you and persecute you and utter all kinds of calumnies against you for My sake.
—Mt 5:11

Do Not Be Discouraged

REFLECTION. Jesus knows when you are hurt, ridiculed, or abandoned because of your faith in Him.

Rejoice and be glad if it happens to you, because they did the same thing to Jesus. The servant cannot be greater than the master.

PRAYER. *Jesus, help me to be meek and humble of heart.*

HENEVER you eat this bread and drink this cup, you proclaim the death of the Lord until He comes.
—1 Cor 11:26

OCT. 13

The Eucharist Will Save You

REFLECTION. The presence of Jesus in the Eucharist is our most precious gift. Attend Mass often to revitalize your spiritual life.

Enjoy the Bread of Angels as you would a king's feast.

PRAYER. *Come into my heart, Lord, and give me strength.*

RAVELING with Him were the Twelve, as well as some women.
—Lk 8:1-2

OCT. 14

Women Cared for Jesus, and He Cared for Them

REFLECTION. We are asked to feed the hungry. What a privilege it was for the women to feed Jesus when He was tired and hungry after a day's travel.

Jesus always loved the women who followed Him.

PRAYER. *Lord Jesus, thank You for loving women; and thank You for loving me.*

HE has done all things well. . . . He even makes the deaf able to hear.

—Mk 7:37

OCT. 15

At Times We Are Deaf

REFLECTION. Some people are in denial about their faults. They are deaf to those who want to help them.

Don't be like them. Listen to those who want to help you.

PRAYER. *Dear God, open my ears that I may hear You.*

"DO NOT be afraid. From now on you will be catching men." . . . they left everything and followed Him.

—Lk 5:10-11

OCT. 16

Do Not Fear Your Weakness

REFLECTION. St. Peter once said, "Depart from me, Lord, for I am a sinful man." Jesus told him not to be afraid of his weakness.

Jesus encouraged Peter. He does the same thing for you.

PRAYER. *Dear Jesus, help me to remember that Your grace is stronger than my weakness.*

HAVE loved you with an everlasting love; I have kept My mercy toward you.

—Jer 31:3

OCT.
17

God Loves His Beloved

REFLECTION. It is almost impossible to fathom God's love for each of us. His love is personal, unconditional, and unchanging.

In fact, His love is His very nature. That's nice to know.

PRAYER. *Lord, I rejoice in the knowledge of Your love and mercy. Never let me forget it.*

 HEY set forth and traveled from village to village, preaching the Gospel and curing diseases everywhere. —Lk 9:6

OCT.
18

Jesus Said: Love, Pray, Go, Teach

REFLECTION. Today is the feast of St. Luke. He reminds us that Jesus said, "Go forth and proclaim the Good News of the Gospel."

You can do that too, in your own way.

PRAYER. *Help me, Lord, to bring Your word to others.*

THE scribes and the Pharisees were very hostile and they began to interrogate Him about many things. —Lk 11:53

OCT. **19**

Be Prepared for Persecution

REFLECTION. This is the feast of St. Isaac Jogues and other martyrs who were his companions.

Hostility toward the Church has been constant since the time of Jesus. Do not be afraid.

PRAYER. *Dear Jesus, give me courage to carry the cross and companions to walk with me.*

WHATEVER you have said in the dark will be heard in the daylight. —Lk 12:3

OCT. **20**

There Are No Secrets from God

REFLECTION. Try to live a straightforward life. Try to avoid secrecy. Open, honest communication with God is the best policy.

Ask God to guide your conscience.

PRAYER. *Holy Spirit of love and truth, help me to be at peace, as I try to do Your Will.*

DO not be concerned about how or what you are to answer or what you are to say. —Lk 12:11

The Holy Spirit Will Be Your Shield

REFLECTION. There are times in life when we are put on the defensive. When that happens let the Holy Spirit speak for you.

He is really there, even though you can't see Him.

PRAYER. *Dear God, I trust You to be my defense in times of need.*

FILL me with Your kindness that I may always shout for joy and gladness. —Ps 90:14

Let a Spirit of Gladness Fill Your Soul

REFLECTION. God's kindness is the basis of human joy.

Believe in God's love, and dedicate yourself to living your life joyfully because of His presence.

PRAYER. *Heavenly Father, I draw strength from Your love, and rejoice in it.*

BE on your guard against all kinds of greed. Life does not depend upon an abundance of one's possessions.

—Lk 12:15

Less Is More

REFLECTION. Greedy people never have enough. Their acquisitive spirit obliterates their peace and joy.

However, those who are generous retain their joy, and they please the Lord in the process.

PRAYER. *Jesus, give me the will to keep my greed in check.*

I HAVE come to spread fire on the earth, and how I wish it were already blazing!

—Lk 12:49

Ask, and the Holy Spirit Will Fill You with Courage

REFLECTION. After the crucifixion the Apostles were frightened and dejected. They gathered in the Upper Room and prayed to the Holy Spirit for strength. All of them were transformed.

PRAYER. *Holy Spirit, light a fire of zeal and courage in my heart; I want to be a Saint.*

FAITH by itself is dead if it does not have works.

—Jas 2:17

OCT. 25

Faith Challenges Us to Pour Out Our Love

REFLECTION. Love involves service, and service requires action. The phrase "faith alone saves" is simply a false teaching.

We must accept Jesus as Lord, and obey Him. Go and love one another.

PRAYER. *Dear Lord, help me to be a doer of Your word and not a hearer only.*

[**T**HE Kingdom of God] is like a mustard seed . . . it grew and became a tree, and the birds of the air made nests in its branches.

—Lk 13:18

OCT. 26

God's Presence Is Always Expanding

REFLECTION. God's love and presence is growing everywhere. Only hatred can keep it from expanding.

Hatred is a form of self-sabotage. Those who hate choose hell over heaven.

PRAYER. *Dear Lord, cleanse me of every trace of hatred in my soul.*

E on your guard lest your hearts be weighed down by carousing and drunkenness and the anxieties of this life.
—Lk 21:34

OCT.
27

You Are Called to Be Holy

REFLECTION. You are a precious creation of the Lord. Follow the blueprint of your maker, and do not give in to your base desires.

You must control your thoughts and desires if you are to find joy.

PRAYER. *Lord, help me to control my unholy yearnings, even if it hurts.*

 DO not understand my own actions. For I do not do what I want; rather, I do what I hate.
—Rom 7:15

OCT.
28

St. Paul Was Human Too

REFLECTION. St. Paul used to say, "When I am weak then I am strong" (2 Cor 12:10). He said this because he knew he couldn't depend on his strength alone, he had to rely on the strength of God.

PRAYER. *Holy Spirit, You are my strength and my joy. I put my trust in You.*

Y house shall be a house of prayer. **OCT.** **29**

—Lk 19:46

Sacred Places Deserve Respect

REFLECTION. We pray best when we enter into God's silence. In church we enter the presence of God.

The only language God speaks is silence. "Be still and acknowledge that I am God" (Ps 46:11).

PRAYER. *Dear Jesus, teach me to be respectful in church and to pray to You always and everywhere.*

———————

 Y brethren, whom I love and for whom I long, my joy and crown: stand firm in the Lord. —Phil 4:1 **OCT.** **30**

God Delights In You

REFLECTION. St. Therese once said, "Everything I have ever done, I have done to make God happy."

It is possible to make God happy simply by responding joyfully to His love.

PRAYER. *Father, I would love to please You more; teach me how to do that.*

NVITE the poor, the crippled, the lame, and the blind. . . . Then indeed will you be blessed. —Lk 14:13-14

OCT. 31

Jesus Lives Mystically in His People

REFLECTION. What you do for the least among us, you do for the Lord. Believe that, and your life will change for the better.

In addition, your eternal happiness will be secured.

PRAYER. *O Divine Physician, help me to see with the eyes of faith. Let me be Your hands and feet in the world.*

 WILL close their wounds and give them health . . . and I will reveal to them the prayer of peace. —Jer 33:6

NOV. 1

God Makes Saints out of Sinners

REFLECTION. Just as God creates out of nothing, He wondrously refines you as pure gold in the "fire," and makes you a Saint-in-training. A Saint suffers some trials and tribulations, but in the process manifests God's love for all to see.

Be patient. Wonderful things are in store for you.

PRAYER. *O Lord, I pray for an increase in the virtue of hope so I may cheer up!*

THE Lord God will wipe away the tears from every cheek. —Isa 25:8

One Day Your Heart Will Sing Again

REFLECTION. Abraham Lincoln once said, "In this sad world of ours, sorrow comes to all. Perfect relief is not possible except with time. You may not believe that you will ever feel better. But this is not true. You are sure to be happy again. Knowing this, truly believing it, will make you less miserable now."

We mourn the loss of those who are dear to us, but as the pain passes, the happy memories remain.

PRAYER. *Dear Lord, heal my soul of its sorrow.*

 WHOEVER keeps My word will never see death. —Jn 8:51

Happy Memories Soothe the Soul

REFLECTION. To cope better with grief, dwell not so much on the feeling of loss; instead think more about the love and laughter you once shared.

You will share them again one day.

PRAYER. *Dear Lord, help me to keep my thoughts from dragging me down. Make me a more joyful person.*

VEN though our outer self is continuing to decay, our inner self is being renewed day by day. —2 Cor 4:16

I Will Use My Gifts and Talents Well

REFLECTION. The best way to keep a piano in good condition is simply to play it. Neglect impairs the instrument in many ways. Tonal quality suffers. The keys turn yellow. The felted hammers become a target for hungry moths.

This scenario is much the same with human beings. If you don't use it, you lose it.

PRAYER. *Dear God, help me to live fully by being spiritually and mentally creative. Help me to do more with my life than merely exist.*

 O NOT fear. . . . When you walk through fire, you shall not be burned. —Isa 43:1, 2

I Have a Mission in Life

REFLECTION. A healthy sense of self is directly related to knowing your mission in life. Your efforts might seem insignificant to you now, but they may be all that is needed to overcome some great evil. Follow your heart.

"It is better to light one candle than to curse the darkness" (Chinese Proverb).

PRAYER. *God in heaven, help me to forget my woes and worries and spend more time on some noble purpose.*

THE mouth speaks from the abundance of the heart.
—Lk 6:45

NOV.
6

Count Your Blessings

REFLECTION. If you were going to die tomorrow and had only one phone call to make, whom would you call? What would you say?

Would you start talking about your sadness, or would you be grateful for all the gifts you received in life?

PRAYER. *Dear Jesus, help me to have a grateful heart.*

I PLACE my trust in You, O Lord. I say, "You are my God." My life is in Your hands.
—Ps 31:15-16

NOV.
7

Each Day Is a Gift

REFLECTION. "One should count each day a separate life" (Lucius Annaeus Seneca).

If you begin your day by trusting God, you will be free of needless worry. Turn all your fears over to the Lord, and He will put a smile on your face.

PRAYER. *Dear Lord, give me the wisdom to enjoy my precious life.*

HELP the poor, and in their need do not send them away empty-handed.

—Sir 29:9

Good Intentions Are the Seeds of Greatness

REFLECTION. You don't have to achieve great things to please the Lord. Come to Him just as you are. He loves His great Saints as well as His little children.

Let Him know about your desire to help others. Dream about becoming a Saint.

PRAYER. *Dear Lord, I want to grow in holiness. Please teach me how.*

 SING and chant . . . giving thanks to God the Father at all times and for everything in the Name of our Lord Jesus Christ.

—Eph 5:19-20

Gratitude Is the Music of the Soul

REFLECTION. Flowers of joy grow out of the garden of gratitude. Be grateful, and your joy will teach you ways to make others a little happier.

A light heart is possible. Count your blessings, and your joy will be complete.

PRAYER. *Dear Lord, help me to be patient with myself when I become moody.*

MEN, amen, I say to you, if you ask the Father for anything in My Name, He will give it to you. . . . Ask and you will receive, so that your joy may be full.

—Jn 16:23-24

You Are Never Alone

REFLECTION. The Lord is with you: when you are sad and tired, when you are feeling useless, when you think you can't go on, and when discouragement clouds your mind.

Remember, Jesus is always standing by your side.

PRAYER. *Lord, lighten up my life with Your joy.*

HIS is the day that the Lord has made; let us exult and rejoice in it.

—Ps 118:24

Today, My Face Will Be More Cheerful

REFLECTION. Did you know that the central message of Christianity is joy?

Pope John Paul II said, "Christ came to bring joy; joy to children, joy to parents, joy to families and friends, joy to the sick and elderly. Christ came to bring joy to all people; go therefore and become messengers of joy."

PRAYER. *Dear Jesus, help me to choose joy as the dominant motif of my life.*

ALLELUIA! Praise, you servants of the Lord, praise the Name of the Lord.
—Ps 113:1

Beauty Is Life-Giving

REFLECTION. Beauty nourishes our souls the way food nourishes our bodies. Search for the beauty that is all around you, and try to see God's face in every person you meet.

" 'Joy' is beholding the beauty of God in all creation" (Blessed Julian of Norwich).

PRAYER. *Dear Lord, help me to see You in everyone I meet.*

JESUS came and proclaimed peace to you who were far away and peace to those who were near.
—Eph 2:17

Let Your Tears Flow

REFLECTION. Tears are good for the soul. Sometimes our disappointments are overwhelming. When you feel your worst, and your tears begin to flow, offer them to the Lord.

"Your tears are collected by the Angels and placed in a golden chalice. You will find them again one day when you present yourself before God" (St. Padre Pio).

PRAYER. *Dear Lord, I offer You all my joys and sorrows.*

F YOUR eyes are sound, your whole body will be filled with light.

—Mt 6:22

Today, I Will Praise More and Complain Less

REFLECTION. Mark Twain said, "I can live for two days on a good compliment." People need affirmation. Why not be more alert to the needs of others.

When you touch them with kindness, they will invite you into their hearts.

PRAYER. *Lord, give me a more loving heart.*

 EE what love the Father has bestowed on us, enabling us to be called the children of God.

—1 Jn 3:1

Feelings Are Not Facts

REFLECTION. God loves you no matter how badly you may feel about yourself. He forgives you no matter how guilty you may feel.

Laugh at your feelings. They are not true.

PRAYER. *Lord, help me to live by faith not by feelings. When I am in darkness I know You are at my side protecting me.*

BIDE in Me, as I abide in you. . . . You cannot bear fruit unless you abide in Me. —Jn 15:4

Live in the Present

REFLECTION. It is only in the present moment that we find true joy. Enjoy your food; enjoy the fresh air you breathe; enjoy your work; and enjoy your leisure time.

The books of wisdom teach us to live in the present moment.

PRAYER. *Dear Lord, give me the grace to live in Your love, while I enjoy my precious life here and now.*

———————

 PRAYED, and understanding was given to me; I pleaded and the spirit of Wisdom came to me. —Wis 7:7

Wisdom Is a Gift

REFLECTION. The most important thing that wisdom can bring us is the knowledge that God is our friend. This friendship is the basis of all our future happiness both here and in heaven.

Start with the firm conviction that God is love. His love for you is personal and eternal.

PRAYER. *Heavenly Father, I thank You for the gift of wisdom.*

KINDLY glance gives joy to the heart, and good news refreshes the bones.

—Prov 15:30

NOV. 18

Learn to Wait

REFLECTION. Winter waits for spring, and spring waits for summer. Everything happens in its proper time. There is no need to force God's timetable.

There is "a time to tear down, and a time to build up. A time to weep, and a time to laugh" (Eccl 3:3-4).

PRAYER. *Dear God, help me to put up with my worrisome mind. Teach me to trust You more.*

 OR everything there is a season, . . . a time to weep, and a time to laugh.

—Eccl 3:1, 4

NOV. 19

Smile, and the World Smiles with You

REFLECTION. After giving a homily on joy, I often give the congregation this advice: "If you have the slightest bit of joy in your heart, please notify your face."

St. Teresa of Avila put it another way, "God, deliver me from sullen Saints."

PRAYER. *Dear Lord, help me to realize that the time to smile is right now.*

HE Kingdom of heaven is close at hand. . . . "Prepare the way of the Lord, make His paths straight." —Mt 3:2-3

Progress Isn't Always What It Seems

REFLECTION. Today you can pull into the driveway, and use a remote control to open the garage door, and a cell phone to announce that you are home.

However, these gadgets cannot help you predict the day or the hour you will be called home to God.

PRAYER. *Lord, help me to be prepared when You call me home.*

LL the believers . . . would sell their property and possessions and distribute the proceeds to all according to what each one needed. —Acts 2:44-45

Christ Is in Your Neighbor

REFLECTION. Jesus is present among us, even though we don't always see Him. Mother Teresa said, "He comes in distressing disguises." Maybe this is why Jesus said, "When I was hungry, did you give Me to eat?" (Mt 25:35).

Pope Benedict XVI said, "Respect for minorities is a clear sign of a true civilization."

PRAYER. *Dear Jesus, give me the eyes to see Your face in everyone.*

IVE thanks to the Lord, for He is good, **NOV.**
for His mercy endures forever.
—Dan 3:89 **22**

Thanksgiving Day Comes Everyday

REFLECTION. Some people believe the first Thanksgiving Feast took place in Massachusetts with the pilgrims and Native Americans. However, it was on October 3, 1863, that Abraham Lincoln declared the fourth Thursday of November as a day for all Americans to thank God for His bountiful blessings.

Lincoln called us "to be humble . . . and implore the Almighty to heal the wounds of the [civil] war."

PRAYER. *Dear Lord, give me a grateful heart.*

 O not judge, so that you in turn may **NOV.**
not be judged.
—Mt 7:1 **23**

Do Not Judge

REFLECTION. You'll feel better if you are ready to give others the benefit of the doubt. Unless you have full access to all the facts, try to withhold your judgment.

Even when the person is truly guilty, remember the words of Jesus, "Father, forgive them, for they do not know what they are doing" (Lk 23:34).

PRAYER. *Dear Lord, make my heart like Yours, that I may be ready to forgive.*

HOEVER gives even a cup of cold water to one of these little ones . . . will not go unrewarded.

—Mt 10:42

Kindness Begets Kindness

REFLECTION. Kindness is its own reward, but when you are kind to others, they will be kind to you in return.

Kindness is a defense against anger, resentment, and bitterness. A gentle spirit better serves your soul and your mental health.

PRAYER. *Dear Lord, help me to attain the gift of sweetness of spirit.*

 AVING endured a slight chastisement, they will receive great blessings, because God tested them and found them worthy to be with Him.

—Wis 3:5

Self-Pity Is Self-Defeating

REFLECTION. The great French artist Renoir suffered so much from arthritis that it was difficult for him to paint. A concerned friend asked him, "Why do you continue to torture yourself?" Renoir replied, "I do it because I know that the pain passes, but the beauty remains."

Find a noble purpose, and your life will transcend the day-to-day drudgery.

PRAYER. *Help me, Lord, to be brave in my times of pain and sorrow.*

HE Word of the Lord is true, and He is faithful in everything He does.

—Ps 33:4

The More You Trust God, the Happier You Will Be

REFLECTION. The great spiritual masters tell us that the path to both happiness and holiness is found in fidelity to the duty of the present moment. If you take care of the little things, the big things will take care of themselves.

Be faithful to the duty of the present moment. Do it for the Lord, and be at peace.

PRAYER. *Lord, I'm such a procrastinator; teach me to be faithful to my duties as they arise.*

 AY the Lord smile upon you and be gracious to you. May the Lord . . . give you His peace. —Num 6:25-26

A Grateful Heart Is a Joy Forever

REFLECTION. Thank the Lord for His truth. Thank Him for your wonderful body, your mind, your heart, and your soul.

Thank Him for the stars in the sky and for planet Earth. Thank Him for your family and friends, and even thank Him for the animals and the flowers.

PRAYER. *Open my eyes, O Lord, to the beauty all around me.*

O NOT lose your confidence now, since your reward will be so great.
—Heb 10:35

The Lord Will Be Your Strength

REFLECTION. St. Paul was knocked off his horse at Damascus, and became a changed man from that moment on.

His act of surrender to the Lord transformed him into a new creation. After his conversion, his strength came from the Lord. So it will be for you.

PRAYER. *Help me to be more confident, Lord. You have become my strength and my joy.*

 NTRUST everything that you do to the Lord, and your plans will turn out to be successful.
—Prov 16:3

The Lord Will Plan Your Day

REFLECTION. If you want to make God laugh, tell Him your plans. The Holy Spirit is living within you. Never think of yourself as one who is entirely alone.

The Lord will be in charge of your coming and going. He will encourage you to be more loving, and He will send a few surprises along the way to keep you docile.

PRAYER. *Dear Lord, help me to listen to Your voice with joyful expectation.*

IVE, and it will be given to you. A good measure, pressed down, shaken together, and running over, will be poured into your lap. —Lk 6:38

Your Generosity Will All Come Back to You

REFLECTION. God works in mysterious ways. What you give to others will return to you one day.

Since you have a debt of gratitude to everyone who ever helped you along the way, express your gratitude while they are still alive, and pray for those who have gone to their eternal rest.

PRAYER. *Lord, help me to be more generous and more grateful.*

 HE God of all consolation . . . consoles us in all our afflictions and thereby enables us to console others in their tribulations. —2 Cor 1:3-4

Think of Yourself As a Healer, Not As a Victim

REFLECTION. Self-pity is the cancer of the soul. You are called to be a healer, not a complainer. Be like Jesus. Think of others.

This is the month of our Savior's birth. Start pondering your mission in life. Call upon the Lord to make you a healer. Begin by canceling any thoughts you have about being a victim. Snap out of it.

PRAYER. *Holy Spirit, soul of my soul, brace me up when I drift into self-pity.*

[ESUS said,] "My Father, if it is not possible for this cup to be taken away unless I drink it, Your Will be done." —Mt 26:42 **DEC. 2**

Jesus Put God's Will before His Own

REFLECTION. By accepting the hand the Father dealt Him, Jesus found His purpose. He took on a burden He didn't especially want to embrace.

He was very human. Nevertheless, He gave up His life that we might live, and used all that pain to purchase our redemption.

PRAYER. *Dear Lord, when life becomes unbearable, remind me of Your spirit of surrender.*

 AY the God of perseverance and encouragement grant that you may live in harmony with one another. —Rom 15:5 **DEC. 3**

Try To See the Face of God in Everyone You Meet

REFLECTION. It isn't easy to do, but you'll be amazed at how seeing God in everyone will change your life. People will start reacting to you in a more pleasant way.

St. Paul asked the Corinthians to greet each other with reverence. This is good advice, since we are all part of the Body of Christ.

PRAYER. *Lord, help me to believe that You are truly present in every person I meet.*

175

THEY surrounded me on every side; in the Name of the Lord I overcame them. —Ps 118:11

Let the Spirit of Jesus Calm the Storm Raging within You

REFLECTION. Foster a calm attitude of mind, even before the trouble begins. You can do this by leaning on the Holy Spirit Who is living within you.

Whenever a panic attack seems imminent, take ten deep breaths, and repeat the words "Thank You, Lord, for keeping me calm."

PRAYER. *Help me, Jesus, to draw my strength from You.*

IF YOU sow generously, you will reap generously as well. —2 Cor 9:6

Love Is Like a Seed

REFLECTION. Love begets more love. It is like the seed that falls on good ground, and grows to produce a rich harvest.

The more love you plant, the greater the harvest. Don't be stingy with your love; you have so much to give, and so much to gain.

PRAYER. *Lord, help me to bear rich and abundant good fruit.*

OU have received the Spirit of adoption, enabling us to cry out, "*Abba! Father!*"
—Rom 8:15

You Are God's Special Child

REFLECTION. Remember that you and Jesus have the same Father. That makes you a special person, an adopted child of God.

Imagine God personally loving you, as any good father would love his only child.

PRAYER. *Father, I rarely feel Your presence, but I know You are there. Bless and comfort me.*

 HEY will be assured that I, the Lord their God, am with them.
— Ezek 34:30

Jesus Was Truly Human

REFLECTION. He was born in an obscure village the child of a peasant woman. . . . He worked in a carpenter shop until He was thirty. For three years He was an itinerant preacher. He never wrote a book. He never held an office.

He was nailed to the Cross between two thieves. . . . When He was dead, He was laid in a borrowed grave through the pity of a friend. More than twenty centuries have come and gone, and today He is still the central figure of the human race. *One Solitary Life*

PRAYER. *Dear Jesus, I bow before You as my Lord and my God.*

IS mother said to the servants, . . . "Do whatever He tells you."

—Jn 2:5

DEC. 8

The Blessed Mother Always Leads Us to Jesus

REFLECTION. Mary's twofold vocation was to bring Jesus into this world, and later to give Him away. At the Lord's first miracle, Mary told Jesus, "They have no more wine." Jesus listened to her, and turned the water into wine.

We honor Mary because Jesus honored her. He even obeyed her.

PRAYER. *Hail Mary, full of grace . . . pray for us now and at the hour of our death.*

 F anyone wishes to boast, let him boast in the Lord.

—1 Cor 1:31

DEC. 9

Humility Is a Form of Honesty

REFLECTION. All your gifts have come from God. Once you admit this, it will be easy to be humble.

All is grace. The only thing you can give to Almighty God that is truly your own, and that He hasn't already given to you, is your trust. Be humble and trust the Lord.

PRAYER. *Dear Lord, this day I place my trust in You.*

HIS is my commandment: love one another as I have loved you.

—Jn 15:12

Love Is Never Easy

REFLECTION. The Russian author Dostoyevski once wrote: "Love is a harsh and dreadful thing." How right he was. True love is in the will. Love often hurts.

Some of your finest moments took place when you made sacrifices for others. The things you did in the name of love will become beautiful jewels in your heavenly crown.

PRAYER. *Lord, help me to keep loving even when it hurts.*

WILL boast most gladly of my weaknesses, in order that the power of Christ may dwell within me.

—2 Cor 12:9

Don't Be Afraid of Your Weakness

REFLECTION. A holy dissatisfaction with self is a good thing. St. Paul boasted of his weakness because it was in weakness that he found God's strength. He came to see that it was God's power in him that made all the difference.

Don't be discouraged because of your weakness. God isn't finished with you yet.

PRAYER. *Teach me to laugh at myself more, O Lord.*

UR competence comes from God Who has empowered us to be the ministers of a new covenant.

DEC.
12

—2 Cor 3:5-6

Honesty Is the Best Policy

REFLECTION. Face it, without God you can do nothing. So when you try to do too much on your own, don't blame anyone else for your failures.

Be honest, make amends, and call on God for help. Once you learn to do that, things will move along a lot smoother for you.

PRAYER. *Lord, give me the grace to see that I am nothing, and You are everything.*

 OUR words . . . became a source of joy to me and the delight of my heart.

DEC.
13

—Jer 15:16

It's a Good Thing to Know Your Limitations

REFLECTION. One of the worst things you can do is overestimate your ability to solve the problems of other people. Meddling can lead to so much needless tension.

Putting your nose in other people's business is not wise. Back off, and wait until you're asked for advice before you give it.

PRAYER. *Lord, Jesus, help me to be wise.*

DO NOT concern myself with great affairs or with things too sublime for me. Rather, I have stilled and calmed my soul.

DEC.
14

—Ps 131:1-2

Do Not Let Your Fears Run Away with You

REFLECTION. The words "Do Not Be Afraid" are repeated 365 times throughout the Bible: first to Isaiah, "Take courage, do not be afraid" (Isa 7:4). The Angel Gabriel said to Mary, "Do not be afraid" (Lk 1:30). Jesus said, "Be not afraid, fear is useless; what you need is trust" (Lk 8:50).

Calm your soul, and be at peace.

PRAYER. *Holy God, I give You all my fears; help me to calm my soul.*

 EJOICE always; . . . for this is the Will of God for you in Christ Jesus.

DEC.
15

—1 Thes 5:16

Cheerfulness Is a Sure Sign of Wisdom

REFLECTION. St. Paul said, "Rejoice always" (1 Thes 5:16). William Shakespeare said, "A light heart lives long."

Jesus explained it this way, "In this world you will have many problems, but be of good cheer for I have overcome the world" (Jn 16:33). Cheerfulness is the sunshine of the soul.

PRAYER. *Dear God, help me to be more light-hearted and happy.*

LOVE one another with genuine affection. Esteem others more highly than yourself.
—Rom 12:10-11

A Friend in Need Is a Friend Indeed

REFLECTION. Did you know that when Mrs. Harry Truman was 18, her father committed suicide? Her friend Mary Paxton came over right away and they talked for hours. Years later, Bess said, "Mary's loving presence was exactly what I needed when I needed it."

People never forget those who reach out to them in their hour of need.

PRAYER. *Jesus, help me to be alert to the needs of others.*

 THE Lord . . . answered me; He set me free from all my fears.
—Ps 34:5

Avoid Self-Sabotage at All Costs

REFLECTION. The Supreme Law is: "Love God, and love your neighbor as you love yourself." This law can be reduced to three simple requirements: cling to God, think of others, and don't put yourself down.

Catch yourself when you begin putting yourself down, and try to become your own best friend.

PRAYER. *Dear God, help me to be kind, above all to myself.*

GIVE joy to the soul of Your servant, for to You, O Lord, I lift up my soul.

—Ps 86:4

Slow Down and Rest in the Lord

REFLECTION. The holiday season can be hectic. Learn to pace yourself. A bird needs its nest, a bee needs its hive, and every human soul needs some pillow talk with God.

St. Augustine said, "Our hearts are restless until they rest in You, O Lord." Resting in God's love, without saying anything, is the purest form of prayer.

PRAYER. *Holy Spirit, help me to enjoy the silence of Your presence.*

THE Kingdom of heaven is like a merchant searching for fine pearls. When he found one of great value, he . . . sold everything he had and bought it.

—Mt 13:45-46

You Are a Pearl of Great Price

REFLECTION. When a speck of sand gets into an oyster, it irritates the flesh around it. To protect itself, the oyster coats it with an iridescent material, so that gradually the grain of sand turns into a beautiful pearl.

You are like a grain of sand. Be patient; God is transforming you into a pearl of great price.

PRAYER. *Thank You, Lord, for purifying me.*

ARY . . . gave birth to Jesus Who is called the Christ.

—Mt 1:16

Jesus Is Your Lord

REFLECTION. The Gospel of Matthew opens with the human genealogy of Jesus. It is a passage that tells of His human roots. He is true God, but true Man as well. He knows what it is to be human; He knows what pain is.

Look to Him for comfort in your distressing moments, and trust that He will be at your side when you need Him.

PRAYER. *Dear Jesus, help me to see You as my dearest friend.*

HE Angel said to him, "Do not be afraid, Zechariah, for your prayer has been heard."

—Lk 1:13

God Answers All Your Prayers

REFLECTION. The demons love to stir up our fears. It's all too human to be afraid, but we are not poor helpless creatures. There is always grace.

Jesus gives us what we need to overcome our apprehensions. He gives us Himself.

PRAYER. *Loving God, with You at my side, I will not be afraid.*

HE Angel came to her and said, "Hail [Mary], full of grace! The Lord is with you." —Lk 1:28

DEC. 22

Mary Is Your Spiritual Mother

REFLECTION. St. Elizabeth said to Mary during the Visitation: "Blessed are you among women and blessed is the fruit of your womb" (Lk 1:42).

These words together with the words of the Angel to Mary and the addition of the name "Jesus" became the first part of the prayer *Hail Mary.*

PRAYER. *Dear Mary, I honor you as the Mother of my Lord, and my Mother.*

Mary Is the Model of Holiness

REFLECTION. Mary has become the prototype of true Christian living because of her perfect compliance with God's Will.

You too are a carrier of God's life wherever you go. Let His light shine forth from you for all to see.

PRAYER. *Lord, I rejoice in the knowledge of Your love.*

WILL offer thanks to the Lord because of His righteousness, and I will sing hymns of praise to the Name of the Lord Most High.

—Ps 7:18

Be Still; the Lord Is Near

REFLECTION. As you anticipate the miracle of His birth, consecrate your life to the Lord. Offer Him your being, and all that you have. Pray for those whom you love.

May the Lord be your strength and your joy in this holy season and always.

PRAYER. *Dear Jesus, I hold You in my heart, and I thank You for Your many gifts.*

 OLY, holy, holy is the Lord of hosts! All the earth is full of His glory.

—Isa 6:3

Make This a Very Merry Christmas

REFLECTION. Lift up your heart and celebrate the great gift of God becoming one of us. The central mystery of the Catholic Church is the Incarnation. God became man.

This means that the glory of the Blessed Trinity dwells among us. We bow in awe before the Infant King.

PRAYER. *Lord, with reverence and love, I rejoice in this day.*

OU will show me the path to life; You will fill me with joy in Your presence.
—Ps 16:11

The Lord Is with You

REFLECTION. Jesus came to us, subject to all the limitations of being human. From the beginning He felt the discomfort of the cold weather, and experienced the pangs of hunger.

His loving Mother shielded Him from needless suffering. She will shield you as well.

PRAYER. *Teach me, Lord, to depend on Your love and Your Mother's love for me.*

 OD brought us to life with Christ . . . and enthroned us with Him in the heavens.
—Eph 2:5-6

Enjoy This Holy Season

REFLECTION. Keep the spirit of Christmas alive in your soul. Live in God's love.

As you begin to make resolutions for the New Year be sure to confess your sins and make a new beginning. Let the assurance of God's protection bring you peace.

PRAYER. *Dear Father, thank You for Your mercy.*

F WE have died with Christ, we believe that we shall also live with Him.

DEC.
28

—Rom 6:8

Jesus Comforts Your Soul with His Love

REFLECTION. Those who rely on the Lord will find joy and consolation in His presence.

Christmas reminds us that the greatest gift we can ever receive is the gift of God's love, which was expressed in the person of Jesus Christ.

PRAYER. *Father, thank You for my faith and my trust in You.*

 HUS there are three things that endure: faith, hope, and love, and the greatest of these is love.

DEC.
29

—1 Cor 13:13

To Be Is to Be Loved

REFLECTION. The Lord was born in a humble stable, and He died on a Cross. His entire life was a gift of love. He wants us to love one another.

To do that we need to be fully aware that we are loved. To be is to be loved.

PRAYER. *Help me, Lord, to know that You love me deeply.*

B E HAPPY. . . . Banish anxiety from your heart and cast off trouble from your presence. **DEC. 30** —Eccl 11:9-10

Jesus Came That Your Joy May Be Full

REFLECTION. Do not let toxic thoughts poison your soul with worry and fear. This season is a time for rejoicing. Let the Lord light up your life.

He will deliver you from evil and bring you the fullness of joy. Anticipate the wonderful gifts that He has in store for you in the New Year.

PRAYER. *Thank You for Your goodness, Lord. Let me greet the year ahead with courage.*

I F YOU have faith as tiny as a mustard seed, you will be able to say to this mountain: "Move from here to there," and it will move. Nothing will be impossible for you. **DEC. 31** —Mt 17:20

God Wants You to Start the New Year with Faith and Courage

REFLECTION. Now that Christmas has come and gone, believe with all your heart in a brighter tomorrow. Pray with real confidence.

Honor the Supreme Intelligence behind all creation. Renew your high hopes for a better future, and the Lord will bless you abundantly.

PRAYER. *Lord, I give myself to You with no restrictions. I am all Yours.*

HOLY WEEK

PALM SUNDAY

ND the crowds that preceded Him and those that followed kept shouting, "*Hosanna* to the Son of David." —Mt 21:9

Lord Save Us

REFLECTION. We are here to profess with victorious vigor that Christ is the Way, the Truth, and the Life.

The explosion of our faith is so strong that— as Jesus said—if our voice were to keep silence, the stones would cry out instead (Pope Paul VI).

PRAYER. *Lord Jesus, I also cry out today with my voice and my heart, "Hosanna, Son of David."* _____

HOLY THURSDAY

OW that I, your Lord and Teacher, have washed your feet, you also should wash one another's feet. —Jn 13:14

Love Your Neighbor

REFLECTION. During the Eucharistic celebration there is the ceremony of the washing of feet. It was the custom to wash the feet of a guest in Jesus' time.

Today it is a sign of our willingness to love and care for our neighbor.

PRAYER. *Lord, make me willing to wash the feet of those who need my love.*

GOOD FRIDAY

AKE up [your] cross and follow Me.

—Mt 16:24

Joy and the Cross Are Not Incompatible

REFLECTION. Good Friday is not an end in itself. It is a gateway to the Resurrection. This means that pain and joy can coexist in your life.

You may be in pain now, but the hope of eternal life informs all our suffering, and gives hope. If you believe it, joy prevails over sorrow.

PRAYER. *Dear Lord, help me to carry my cross with courage.*

HOLY SATURDAY

ECAUSE of the Preparation Day of the Jews, they laid Jesus in a new tomb in which no one had yet been laid. —Jn 19:41-42

Our New Life in Christ

REFLECTION. The readings in the Paschal Vigil carry us into the mysterious arena where human sin meets God's justice and mercy.

There life and death "have contended," and there the victory of the risen Christ over death stands out as the source of our salvation and the model of Christian living (Pope Paul VI).

PRAYER. *Lord, as we await in silence the outpouring of joy with which we will celebrate Your Resurrection, help me to prepare diligently.*

EASTER SUNDAY

 E have placed our hope in the living God.

—1 Tim 4:10

Cherish the Promise of Salvation

REFLECTION. Every Easter, "we celebrate the greatest and most shining feast" (St. John Chrysostom). But this celebration is not merely an annual event.

"We are an Easter people and alleluia is our song," (St. Augustine). The whole Christian life is about joyful expectation.

PRAYER. *Dear God, fill me with the joy that comes from the knowledge of Your love.*

OTHER OUTSTANDING CATHOLIC BOOKS

WORDS OF COMFORT FOR EVERY DAY—Short meditation for every day including a Scripture text and a meditative prayer to God the Father. Printed in two colors. 192 pages. **No. 186**

LEAD, KINDLY LIGHT—By Rev. James Sharp. Minute meditations for every day of the year taken from the writings of Cardinal Newman plus a concluding prayer for each day. **No. 184**

EVERY DAY IS A GIFT—Introduction by Most Rev. Frederick Schroeder. Popular meditations for every day, featuring a text from Sacred Scripture, a quotation from the writings of a Saint, and a meaningful prayer. **No. 195**

MARY DAY BY DAY—Minute meditations for every day of the year, including a Scripture passage, a quotation from the Saints, and a concluding prayer. Printed in two colors with over 300 illustrations. **No. 180**

MINUTE MEDITATIONS FROM THE POPES—By Rev. Jude Winkler, O.F.M. Conv. Minute meditations for every day of the year using the words of twentieth-century Popes. Printed and illustrated in two colors. **No. 175**

AUGUSTINE DAY BY DAY—By Rev. John Rotelle, O.S.A. Minute meditations for every day of the year taken from the writings of Augustine, with a concluding prayer also from the Saints. **No. 170**

BIBLE DAY BY DAY—By Rev. John Kersten, S.V.D. Minute Bible meditations for every day including a short Scripture text and brief reflection. Printed in two colors with 300 illustrations. **No. 150**

MINUTE MEDITATIONS FOR EACH DAY— By Rev. Bede Naegele O.C.D. This very attractive book offers a short Scripture text, a practical reflection, and a meaningful prayer for each day of the year. **No. 190**

LIVING WISDOM FOR EVERY DAY—By Rev. Bennet Kelley, C.P. Choice texts from St. Paul of the Cross, one of the true Masters of Spirituality, and a prayer for each day. **No. 182**

www.catholicbookpublishing.com

ISBN 978-1-937913-02-1

90000